KT-592-376

A Colourful Canvas

Twelve Women Artists
in the
North West

Judy Rose
Wendy J Levy

WJL

First published in 2006 by
Wendy J Levy Contemporary Art Ltd.,
17 Warburton Street,
Didsbury, Manchester.
M20 6WA
www.wendyjlevy-art.com

© Judy Rose, Wendy J Levy and the artists

ISBN 0 9549074 2 6

British Library Cataloguing-in-Publication Data.
A catalogue record for this book is available from the British Library.

All rights reserved. No part of this publication may be reproduced, stored in a retrieval system, or transmitted, in any form or by any means, electronic, mechanical, photocopying, recording or otherwise, without the prior consent of the publishers.

Produced by Sansom and Company Ltd, Bristol.
Design and typesetting by Stephen Morris Communications, smc@freeuk.com
Printed by HSW Print (01443) 441100

Contents

Foreword

IN ONE OF THE VERY GREAT VICTORIAN NOVELS, there occurs an unforgettable image. It is night. A woman standing by a window holds up a candle as she looks out into the blackness. The panes of the window reflect her face. As she looks she sees not out of but into the window: the candle-light registers the stresses and strains of its facture and weathering, creating a spider's web of craquelatures, quivering silver against black. As she looks, she imagines these lines as the connecting threads that link together the lives of those that make up her world – all brought together by invisible pathways to this moment, this place.

This book operates in a similar manner; in these pages, drawn together from across the world, twelve women artists are each represented by a short essay and a selection of their works. The paintings, drawings and sculptures found here are all responses to their individual narratives – the stories they have woven from their lives, presented here for us to share. In a world dominated by the constant bombardment on our senses from every conceivable quarter these works offer an opportunity for a willed encounter, one that may last a few seconds or one that perhaps may continue for a lifetime. Works of art are still – they don't change, but we do. It is one of the defining aspects of art that, in a shifting world, it can act as a constant companion, accompanying us through our lives, acting as the candle-light reflected in the darkened window – it at once reveals something of ourselves and the world beyond us.

These works act as so many strands of a web. They weave together a shared narrative of how we can understand the world and our place within it. Each work of art, whether it be paint on canvas, a piece of chiselled stone or the graphic marks of pencil or charcoal preserve the trace of an individual human being's response to experience. All deal with the age-old principle that lies at the heart of what it is to be human: our need to tell stories, to move from the private to the public, to communicate and to make visible. We need such people.

Michael Howard
Art historian and artist
Manchester Metropolitan University

▨ Introduction

IN THE NORTHWEST OF ENGLAND THERE IS AN
ABUNDANCE OF ARTISTIC TALENT, flourishing
in both men and women. In this book, I have
chosen to concentrate on a small, select
group of women artists, who have lived in
various parts of the world, but now find
themselves living and working in the regions
of Manchester and Cheshire. There are very
many more women artists whose talents are
worthy of inclusion and it is my regret that
all are not embraced and celebrated within
this volume.

Wendy J Levy

Michael Kennedy, 2006, 60 x 30 x 36, bronze. Photo by Gerald Hoberman

Cecile Elstein

'My earliest significant memory was when I was about four or five years old. I was walking with my mother down a tree lined, sun filtered gravel path. Now and again I jumped in and out of the sharp diagonal shadows made by the sun. As I kicked the gravel with my foot in its loose, well scuffed, once brown leather sandal, I noticed a perfectly oval, white little stone and picked it up. The smooth pebble fitted in the palm of my hand. I pulled at my mother's softly pleated beige skirt and, as she walked, her skirt caught the sunlight and shades as rhythm. I interrupted this double pattern, one hard-edged and still and the other softly moving, by catching her attention and showing her the pebble.' Thus Cecile Elstein describes an early moment of her heightened awareness of her surroundings and the way in which that awareness is linked to vision, movement, rhythm and wonder. In that early experience the will to communicate the significance of a precious moment began.

Born in 1938 in Cape Town, South Africa, Cecile Hoberman enjoyed a mainly outdoor life at the foot of Table Mountain. She recalls strong visual images and the patterns made by the powerful sun on the sea, the forests and rocks. The mountain roads cut into the mountainside provided Cecile with her first artistic material; making mud pies from the many different colours of the mud strata of the mountain revealed as horizontal layers where the mountain met the road. This was an early opportunity to play through the manipulation of material, an ever present and vital aspect of her art.

Other strong childhood images remain. As a young girl of eleven, she recalls walking along with her younger brother to the local art gallery where the gloomy interior contrasted sharply with the bright sunshine outside, and coming upon a Rodin bronze about fifteen inches high titled *Brother and Sister*. Rodin's sculpture of a girl sitting with her younger brother on her lap was a pose that mirrored Cecile's love for her little brother. For the first time she understood that emotion could be constructed through material into form.

As a young girl at school she gravitated towards the art room where the progressive American art teacher laid out an array of materials and still-life objects

Photo by Michael Pollard
and Peter Burton

including bowls of tropical fruits to encourage self-discovery and experimentation. Art was not considered an exam-worthy subject, so Cecile was able to explore the forms with paint and brushes on paper without constraint, direction or examination. The early experience of the value of self-directed learning and freedom to learn, is a key factor in understanding her approach to her work and to her philosophy of life.

Cecile's parents did not feel that art was a valid profession but, whilst working as a research technician in a medical laboratory, Cecile had a strong conviction to study sculpture. Her weekend teacher, Nel Kaye, taught her how to look at her subject, the basics of anatomy, and proportions. During this period she produced her first sculptures, often of family members, where she was able to experiment with finding ways to capture the essence of the person. She discovered that in talking to her sitters informally and encouraging them to move about freely, she was able to establish a connection and explains that a portrait bronze is the result of the flow of attention between the sitter, the artist and the material.

After her marriage to Max Elstein, Cecile moved to Stellenbosch, a beautiful wine-growing area of South Africa 30 miles from Cape Town, and set up a studio at home. There she met the painter, Neville Lewis who taught her drawing. She attended the Michaelis School of Art in Cape Town, travelling by train very early in the morning. Here her sculpture was directed by Lippy Lipschitz and Mitford Barbeton. In 1960 while living in Stellenbosch, Cecile modelled a portrait of Bengi Champion, the fourteenth child of a couple who lived on a local farm. The iniquities that this family suffered from the draconian apartheid laws were acutely understood. In Bengi's face one can see Cecile's love, acceptance and appreciation of different cultures, along with the child's own pride, composure and resilience in the face of adversity. In this piece of sculpture, one can read Cecile's openness to experience, her tolerance and her desire and ability to connect with people.

Stellenbosch, a Nationalist stronghold, was politically not a comfortable place to live in at this time. Not wanting to bring up a family there, Cecile and Max left in 1961 and arrived in London to face the huge challenge of adapting to a different culture and environment. London, though, was very exciting: politics, art and music presented within a new wave of openness that had not been experienced before.

In London she met Catherine Yarrow, a ceramist who knew Giacometti and had worked with the potter Jose Llorens Artigas, who had collaborated with Miro and Picasso to produce their ceramics. Artigas's *Formulario y practicas de Ceramica* formed the basis of glaze-making for Cecile under the direction of Catherine. Catherine Yarrow took very few pupils and Cecile feels, to this day, privileged to have studied with Yarrow, believing that, through ceramics, she learned vital lessons about creativity. Allowing Cecile complete freedom in her creations, Catherine would not comment on her work; she would simply look at it and then write down what was to be done for the following week. While this was at times frustrating for Cecile, it also gave her the opportunity to continue on her own path and to develop confidence. Cecile also grew to understand the value of total acceptance in relationships. Yarrow's teaching methods were, in part, influenced by her friend, Bunty Wills, a Jungian psychotherapist who specialised in creativity in London during the sixties.

In 1965 Cecile sculpted the portrait of Pinchas Lavon. Coming face to face with one of her bronze portrait sculptures is akin to discovering profound and universal human truths; truths which link us to our past, our future, each other and to the suffering of humanity. Pinchas Lavon was the Minister of Agriculture and Defence under Prime Minister David Ben Gurion in Israel during the early 1950s. He sat for Cecile over three days while in England, his career having ended after his forced resignation following an incident in which many believe he had been falsely implicated. In his face one can see and feel his suffering, his pride and love for his country. One can also see Cecile's empathy towards him. She recalls seeing Donatello's *Mary Magdalene* in Florence and marvelling at the way in which his wonderful skill in carving is informed by his psychological insight of the subject. It is this fusion that Cecile admires and strives for in her own work.

In stark contrast to 'Pinchas Lavon' and his sadness and disappointment, is *Head of a Young Girl*. The bronze portrait represents a universal image of a young girl: searching, optimistic, brightly looking into the future with everything to discover. Later, a bronze cast of a bookstand was used as a plinth for this sculpture in order to portray youth as an open book.

In *Head of a Young Girl* Cecile sought to represent universal youth, but in *Maureen*, a bronze portrait sculpture of her daughter, Cecile sought to understand realistic characteristics and qualities.

In 1970, the family moved from London to Southampton where she received several commissions for portrait bronzes and exhibited at the Society of Portrait Sculptors in London. During her time in Southampton, Cecile met and worked with many other artists, exploring various media through which to express her ideas. Her collaboration with the painters Frank Spears, also recently from South Africa, Molly Dicker, Peter Faulkes and Clive Daley proved particularly rewarding, firing her creativity and energy and becoming an important conduit for further development. In Southampton, Cecile made a bronze portrait of Professor David Millar, who was terminally ill at the time. They spoke together for many hours during the making of this portrait which shows David both as the stoical soldier he had once been with

Bengi Champion, 1960, bronze,
45 x 16 x 29cms

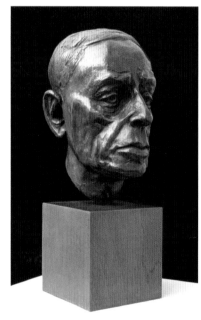

Pinchas Lavon, 1964, bronze,
46 x 21 x 25cms

a courageous expression, and also as a kindly yet vulnerable human being. The sculpture, sited in Southampton Medical School, was stolen. While all assumed that the theft had been prompted by greed and the intention to sell it for scrap, the reality was very different. The piece was actually taken by someone who worked in the University simply because he loved it and wanted to see it every day. Guilt, however, eventually surfaced and the portrait was returned as the perpetrator felt that David's eyes were 'too much on him!' After a letter of apology to David's widow, the incident was put to one side. This surely is a powerful testament to Cecile's work.

Always thirsty for knowledge, spurred on by the need to learn and the will to take charge of her own development, Cecile embarked upon a BA in Sculpture and Printmaking at West Surrey College of Art and Design between 1975 and 1977.

It was there that her tutor, the sculptor, Ian Walters, introduced Cecile to the head teacher of The Florence Treloar School in Alton, Surrey, a boarding school for physically disabled children, who invited her to provide 'something sculptural' for the children to use in their grassy playground. In preparing her thoughts for this project and to get to know the children, she spent much time talking with them, encouraging them to share their interests and views. On hearing that the children had been reading about tree houses, but with their disabilities would have been unlikely ever to have experienced the joy and fun of climbing up to one, Cecile came up with the idea of a structure that would capture the magic of a tree house, but would be accessible to all children. The structure would also accommodate their wheelchairs, allowing the children greater independence, imagination, and drama. Cecile felt that the structure should behave like a tree

Head of a Young Girl, 1973, bronze, 45 x 25 x 32cms. Photo by Reginald Harris

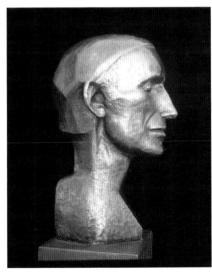

David Millar, 1971, bronze, 50 x 33 x 29cms

house, being a private space away from the main school building, with the rough and smooth textures of a tree. Her great skill as a sculptor enabled her to bring the tree house concept down to earth for these children, giving them the chance to explore imaginative play and to challenge the environment within the limits of their physical capabilities. A totally liberating environment, the horizontal, vertical and diagonal lines of the structure came together to form a double helix, a strong and symbolic image, open, sheltering and nurturing.

When Cecile moved to Manchester in 1978, she set up her workshop in Didsbury and began to work on The Sisyphus Suite, a piece of work comprised of eight separate images, inspired by Albert Camus' explanation of the Myth of Sisyphus. The myth is seen as a metaphor for existence, inviting one to live and create in the midst of adversity. These images were printed at the Manchester Print Workshop by the master printmaker, Kip Gresham. Wanting to further explore the medium of printmaking, Cecile began a creative relationship with Kip, a collaboration that was to prove immensely fruitful for many years.

During the 1980s Cecile was invited to teach ceramics and drawing to community groups such as the families of disabled children in Ancoats and mentally disabled people in Fallowfield.

Cecile's observations of the contemporary mother child relationship can be seen in *Isobel with Children*. This bronze sculpture portrays a nurturing, protecting mother, with her two children. 'In this archetypal image, one feels the essence of them being together while each person retains an individ-

Isobel with Children. Photo by Gerald Hoberman

Play structure

uality: this sculpture is a comment on the need children have to grow and develop independently while still being protected and nurtured.

In 1984 Cecile was awarded a bursary by North West Arts to develop a new modular chamber titled Mandarah, an air supported sunlit colour and sound environment at Manchester Art and Technology Workshop with Terry Scales. It is described in the catalogue, *Dance Performance Spheres of Influence*, as follows: 'Mandarah is spaces and places for people, for performance and interpretations; a sanctuary for ritual, or a playhouse for mime, where the performance is often the actions and reactions of the audience reflecting the exuberance and energy released by the power of colour as experienced within the structure.' 'Mandarah' was exhibited nationally and at the Singapore Arts Festival 1986.

The *Morning, Noon* and *Evening Meetings* were editioned in 1984. These three large screenprints, each of three women in conversation, represent the passage of time by changing light on their forms and the rays of the sun which move around the printed 'frame' of each image. Cecile's love of colour, celebrated by the Meetings was rewarded in 1986 when she received the Sericol Colour Prize at the Bradford International Print Biennale for *Noon Meeting*.

During this time Cecile's work underwent stylistic changes. In 1985, the family was devastated by the news that their son, Paul, who had recently graduated from Oxford, had multiple sclerosis. The art school which she had started with a number of other artists was given up so that she could care for her son. Wanting to be as independent as possible, Paul moved to his own home in Derbyshire and Cecile set up a network of support and care and helped him to reconstruct his house for wheelchair use.

Cecile worked on short-term projects that she could complete whilst caring for Paul. Her printmaking with Kip took on a special quality; profound, quick, spontaneous pieces, some of which recounted happier periods in her life. This affirmation and acknowledgement of past good times in a period of desolation became an essential part of her creative adaptation to cope with what she was facing. Her immense generosity of spirit also enabled her to work with other disabled groups in the community, teaching them to draw and producing a carer's guide that could be distributed by district nurses and general practitioners to others coping with disability.

In 1987, Cecile's stylistic changes within the medium of printmaking culminated in the 'Overflowing Knots and Colour' series. 'Her screenprints are built up from superimposed layers of colour. Since the images are built up from transparent layers that affect and enhance each other, each layer adds to and enriches what lies below. No layer destroys what lies beneath; each layer adds meaning to what has gone before', said Sarah Hyde in the leaflet, *A Printmaking Partnership Cecile Elstein Kip Gresham*, published by Manchester's Whitworth Art Gallery in 1991, the year in which Cecile's collaboration with Kip culminated in an exhibition at the gallery, where she acknowledged the huge role that Kip had played in her creative growth. His technical expertise had enabled her to produce an exciting body of work. This kind of symbiotic relationship has been the foundation of many creative partnerships. In her book, *Exhibiting Gender*, 1997, Sarah Hyde discusses the way in which the growing technical complexity of printmaking means that the end result is made 'not by the hand of a single artist, but as the result of a complex collaborative process', where each discipline informs the other and the whole becomes much more than the sum of its parts.

In 1993 Cecile's interest in the environment led her to embark upon an M.A. 'Art as Environment' within the Department of Art and Design at Manchester University. Her dissertation, *The Role of Empathy in Design Education*, was born out of her interest and understanding of the needs of the disabled. At that time, buildings were often designed without disabled people in mind. Her dissertation is now in the library of the Centre for Accessible Environments in London.

In 1996 Cecile was invited to produce a sculpture for a temporary exhibition at The

Noon Meeting, 1984, screen print on Arches, 85 x 76cms. Photo by Miki Slingsby

Open House, 1988, screen print on
Arches, 120 x 91cms.
Photo by Miki Slingsby

*Together with
Tangents* and *Evie
Garrett, 1996-97.*
Photo by Ron
Kleinman

National Trust's Wimpole Hall Gardens in Cambridgeshire. Other sculptors included Henry Moore, Kenneth Armitage, Rick Kirby, Sophie Ryder and Lida Cordoza-Kindersleigh. The gardens, designed by 'Capability' Brown, and the surrounding Cambridgeshire wheat fields, invoked a memory for Cecile of Gustave Courbet's 1855 painting *The Corn Sifters* which she had seen at the Royal Academy of Arts in 1978. The painting was to become the inspiration for her temporary installation, titled *Together with Tangents*.

Courbet used vanishing lines to create space. He views, from above, the scene of a young woman kneeling on the ground, winnowing corn through a sieve. Her strong arms hold the oval sieve in tension parallel with the ground upon which the sieved wheat falls lightly. Our attention is drawn to her connection with the earth. Cecile says of this painting

> Courbet's woman places her knees apart on the ground, forming a structure of balance and energy. Inspired by the stable feeling of this physical structure, I designed the metal stakes for my sculpture so that they would remain firmly rooted and hold ropes above the ground, forming parallel planes with the changing surface of the growing grass during the summer.

This temporary, site-specific, rope and metal construction, inspired by adaptation towards growth and change, focuses on the values of open relationships with the environment and with others. This open form of sculpture – a comment on Cecile's view of the cyber world and the times we live in – was partly inspired by her son's courageous and open response to his disability.

During the exhibition at Wimpole Hall Gardens, Cecile invited members of the public to respond to *Together with Tangents* and she observed the way in which people's action in their own life experiences informed their interpretation. 'A telephone engineer said that it was obviously about communication; a lace maker thought that the tensions and fixings were like lace-making; a musician saw the structure of music; a writer described the structure of language, and so on.' In this way, Cecile believes that sculptural forms can trigger memories and empathy as people seek to understand each other's responses.

Cecile's interest in architectural and mathematical principles is evident. A strong influence on her work is Buckminster Fuller: inventor, architect, engineer, mathematician, poet and cosmologist, whose ideas were concerned with maximising the potential of every human being, and preserving 'Planet Earth', an idealistic system of thought based on the essential unity of the natural world. One may not immediately link the disciplines of sculpture and mathematics, but in Cecile's studio the connection is apparent. In preparation for *Together with Tangents*, meticulous, geometric drawings were produced. A huge protractor hangs on

Paul, 1983, plaster.
Photo by Gerald Hoberman

the wall; angles were measured and recorded and scaled structures were made. The experience of producing *Together with Tangents* had far-reaching ramifications and was ultimately to lead Cecile into all kinds of different projects. In 1997, Cecile was elected fellow of the Royal Society of Arts.

The following year Paul David Elstein passed away. Cecile's photographs of a plaster portrait of her son, done in preparation for a bronze, are precious. Unfortunately, the bronze sculpture didn't materialise because the model was accidentally ruined in the foundry. The photographs are all that remain.

In the year 2000 Cecile began a project with her film-maker daughter, Maureen Kendal, to produce two films based on their shared experiences of *Together with Tangents* in the context of Wimpole Hall Gardens. The first film, *Tangents, a Mindscape or a Load of Rope?* brings together the concept, drawing and models of the sculpture as it was being developed, together with dialogues from members of the viewing public. The second film, *Present*, completed in 2003, alludes to being in the present rather than to represent. The music was composed for *Present* by the contemporary composer Paul Clay.

Forever active, Cecile Elstein, with fibre artist Margaret Crowther, founded Didsbury Drawing in 2001. A group of up to fourteen local artists who, to the present day, come together regularly to draw from a model. In this unique, democratic and non-profit-making environment the artists experiment and draw from the model without the need to see each other's work. In this uninhibited atmosphere each has the time and space to build a personal visual language.

Michael Kennedy, writer and music critic for the *Daily Telegraph* for many years, was the subject of a bronze portrait completed by Cecile in 2005. The sculpture was commissioned to celebrate his 80th birthday. Cecile has revealed the essence of the sitter. She says, 'A portrait is a time stone.' The modelling material she chooses for a portrait sculpture is often dependent on the characteristics of the sitter. Classical, still faces would dictate using plaster which can be carved rather than modelled, but if the sitter is mobile and animated Cecile may

Dream, edition II, 2005, bronze on wood, 86 x 47 x 41cms. Photo by Gerald Hoberman

choose to use clay to facilitate rapid changes.

Her current work includes several sculpture projects that are waiting her attention, and a series of drawings of four music lovers. They had formed a group to share their love of music with Paul during the time that he became progressively disabled. Cecile now feels she would like to get to know them better. She says, 'since we all carry the whole of our experience within ourselves the final image is a result of the artist's connection with the sitter's experience, not only a copy of the face.'

Sculptors have to possess and contain opposing forces in their make-up. The openness to experience, compassion and empathy – characteristics which Cecile has in abundance and which shine through in her work – are grounded in the everyday practical hard graft of producing a sculpture. The huge array of tools, the logs of wood, bags of clay and coils of wire all remind us that this is very disciplined hard work and to excel at it the sculptor must possess a variety of technical skills. Cecile believes in action and she quotes the Japanese potter, Shoji Hamada, who when asked, 'How do you make your pots?' answered, 'I just do it.'

Cecile traces her satisfaction in grappling with materials from her childhood days of making mud pies, a pursuit continued well after childhood. Part of the pleasure lies in discovering the nature and properties of the material with which she is working. She likens this to meeting someone new, when one is trying to get to understand their characteristics and the shape of the potential relationship with its strengths, limitations and constraints.

John Garfield, 1990, bronze.
Photo by Gerald Hoberman

The preparation of the clay is a pleasure for Cecile. She prepares it as a potter would, wedging it by hand, throwing it on a board and cutting it over and over again until the bubbles have disappeared. She loves the contact with natural earthy material and quotes the art critic Peter Fuller who said in 1976, 'materials and mankind are both derivatives of matter; without this tight attachment to materials and without interest in their existence the rise of our whole culture and civilisation would have been impossible.' It is through this connection with materials that mankind has been able to make sense of the world.

Cecile's connection with materials is apparent on entering her studio. Pieces of charcoal, found during a walk, have been used to give life to a drawing. A huge piece of elm lies on a table; it is being carved into an archetypal image, that of a person resting their forehead on an upraised arm. She takes huge pleasure in the tools of her trade and enthuses over the way in which a particular swivel knife works. She marvels at her array of wood-carving tools and the way in which tools from different countries mirror that country's national characteristics.

Whatever the material, whether Cecile is sculpting, drawing, making films or printing, her motivation is firmly focused on connecting with the environment. With a passion for life, however difficult things are, she says, 'The quality of being, that is emotion, intellect and spirit, is made evident in the action of making art.'

Georgie, Supai limestone, 143 x 91 x 78cms. Collection of Nicola Horlick. Photo by Nigel Hillier

DAWN ROWLAND

Dawn Rowland describes her sculptures as her 'emotional c.v.' in which she openly expresses her feelings about being a woman, a mother, a daughter, and a wife. In short, her work is about relationships and life-experiences. It is charged with intense emotion and executed with extraordinary skill.

Dawn Shane was born with her twin brother, Barry, in 1944 in London. She was the older twin and she now jokingly remarks, 'It's the only time Barry ever said to me "Ladies First".' As a child, Dawn was acknowledged by her parents as the artist of the family and Barry as the scientist, roles they both fulfilled as adults. Encouraged by her creative mother to develop her talents, Dawn attended evening classes in order to pursue the study of art.

In 1965 she married Malcolm Rowland whose post-doctoral research took them to San Francisco, supposedly for one year. They stayed for ten years, bringing up their two small daughters there. San Francisco offered Dawn her first real chance to pursue a more creative path. Whilst the girls, Lisa and Michelle, were babies, she found time to take up life drawing classes near their home in Marin County across the Golden Gate Bridge. Attending a charity coffee morning in the form of a 'clay-in' to raise funds for the San Francisco Symphony Orchestra, Dawn had her first experience of modelling a piece of clay. She immediately loved its tactile quality and the sensation of working in three dimensions. Her piece of work was donated to raise funds for the charity, and sold immediately.

In 1974, Malcolm's career brought the family back to London for a year, at the end of which, Dawn was to have a significant and life-changing experience. On arriving in London, she decided she wanted to take sculpture classes and enrolled at Camden Arts Centre where she began modelling in clay and drawing from a life model. At the end of the year, a two-week course in stone carving was advertised. Dawn enrolled and thus began her lifelong love affair. From the first moment that she held a mallet in one hand and a chisel in the other, all her instincts and emotions told her that this was what she was destined to do.

Her first piece of sculpture was carved in white alabaster. Initially intimidated by the enormity of transforming this nondescript block into a work of art, Dawn spent the first two days just looking at it, trying to imagine what the finished piece might be. Referring to her own experiences and emotions, the alabaster became a mother and child, the two entwined forms depicting a total involvement with each other.

The Warrior Dreams...His Mother Waits, 1996, bronze, 51 x 54 x 26cms. Edition of 6, 2 in private collections in UK and USA. Photo by Steve Russell

After the year in London, the family moved back to San Francisco for what was to be its final year there before a planned move to Manchester. This proved to be a wonderful and inspirational year for Dawn. Determined to explore and develop her new-found vocation, she searched for sculpture classes and found, close to their home, an atelier run by Guy Schwartz, a sculptor from New York. He was an excellent teacher, encouraging Dawn to explore and exploit her own creativity. Under his gentle guidance her confidence and ability blossomed.

On arrival in Manchester in 1975, Dawn's prime concern was to continue stone carving. Again, she joined life drawing and modelling courses where she drew and sculpted from the model in order to glean as much anatomical information as she could in her quest to perfect the skill of accurately recreating the human figure. By 1976 she had her own studio where she worked in stone with dedication and enthusiasm in the development of her work, which

An Emotional Year, 1995, alabaster, 56 x 87 x 25cms. Photo by Ian Tilton

My Sister... Myself, 2003, bronze, 56 x 118 x 30cms. Photo by Steve Russell

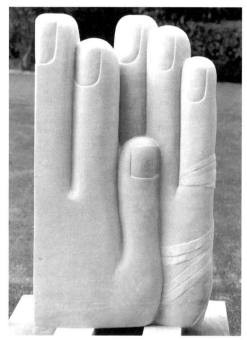

Letting Go, 1996, Indiana limestone, 112 x 69 x 46cms. Photo by Ian Tilton

resulted in her being elected a Member of the Manchester Academy of Fine Arts in 1977, and a Council Member from 1980–1999. She was a member of the Selection Committee and the Hanging Committee for many years.

Her work is predominantly based on the human form, or some part of it, especially heads and hands which she finds most expressive. Dawn continues, to this day, to regard drawing as an important and fundamental part of her work. She produces very impressive life drawings, some larger than life and twice as powerful. However, she doesn't use preliminary sketches when making her carvings, preferring to draw directly onto the stone, changing the form if necessary as the work progresses. Nor does she use a maquette, a preliminary small-scale model upon which to base the sculpture. This style of working explains much about Dawn; her work is intuitive, expressive and emotional and would be too constrained by the process of working from a maquette. Her preferred materials are marble, limestone, alabaster and soapstone, sometimes having selected pieces cast in bronze if she thinks they will work well in that medium.

Father and Son, 1990, limestone, 138cms tall. Collection Jeffrey Archer.
Photo by Ian Tilton

She has always been, and continues to be, exhilarated by the exciting process of working with a piece of stone and watching her emotions gradually emerge as a tangible image. She is so emotionally connected to her work that creating a piece of sculpture is rather like giving birth. Of the immense satisfaction that Dawn derives from working with stone, she says, 'I even love the pain that inevitably must come with this pleasure.' Carving stone is an arduous task that requires an enormous amount of physical effort and concentration, not to mention great skill and time; one false move with the chisel could have a devastating effect, obliterating weeks, if not months, of hard work.

The 1980s saw a steady development of Dawn's recognition as a sculptor. In 1983 she had her first solo exhibition at the Pitcairn Galleries in Knutsford, Cheshire, and in 1984 a solo exhibition at Salford Art Gallery. In 1985 she became a Member of the National Artists

Association. In the same year she was awarded the Coopers & Lybrand Award for the piece of sculpture included in the Manchester Academy of Fine Arts Exhibition. Her third solo show took place in 1986 at the Ginnel Gallery in Manchester and in the same year she gained the National Westminster Bank Award for her exhibit at the Manchester Academy of Fine Arts. Throughout the 1980s her work was exhibited in galleries throughout the country, including several in London. During this period her work was also exhibited on three occasions at the Royal Academy Summer Exhibition in London.

The 1990s were no less eventful for Dawn; in 1991 she was made a member of the Royal Society of British Sculptors (now the Royal British Society of Sculptors), and was elected a Fellow in 1994. She was a Council Member from 1993 to 1999 and was re-elected to the Council in 2006. She was presented to the Queen at the opening of the Royal British Society's International Sculpture Exhibition, 'Chelsea Harbour Sculpture 1993'. Her impressive 138 cm limestone carving entitled *Father and Son* was purchased by Jeffrey Archer. Although Dawn doesn't have any sons, she enjoys expressing, through her sculptures, the relationship between father and son. In Mediterranean cultures, an outward show of affection between men is quite common. Here however, it is more unusual and in *Father and Son* Dawn portrays this special bond as the boy's head nestles tenderly against the father's strong and protective shoulder.

A major solo exhibition of Dawn's work took place at the end of 1993 and the beginning of 1994 at the Konishi Gallery in Kyoto, Japan. One of the pieces entitled *The Silent Scream* aroused the curiosity of a Japanese visitor who wanted to know the meaning of the title. Dawn explained that the sculpture depicts one of those moments of intense frustration experienced by most women, when there is so much to deal with, and so much going on, that there is a need to retreat somewhere private and scream, but with our social conditioning, no sound comes out. The Japanese woman smiled empathetically; the sculpture bridged the cultural divide. In the year 2000, a large and important retrospective exhibition of Dawn's work was curated by Davies and Tooth at the Air Gallery on Dover Street, London. The exhibition attracted critical acclaim.

Dawn's intuitive understanding of her own emotions has been fundamental to the production of her sculptures. Often working in a series, with a number of variations and sequences, Dawn explores a range of emotions until the theme comes to its natural conclusion. However, she may find herself returning to those issues several years later, as she explains, 'I suppose the basic sentiments underlying my work are part of me and therefore can never be totally resolved.'

Letting Go worked in Indiana limestone is one such series which explores the feelings that arise when a child leaves home. The mother's hands are raised to gently push the child forward towards a new life – to let go – but are still there to cushion and protect if necessary. The child's head is wrapped with a blindfold, covering the child's eyes; this blindfold is often used by Dawn to denote the unseeing innocence of childhood as the young ones venture out into an unknown world. Dawn says 'parts of the blindfold are still attached to the mother's hands. That is because mothers never really, totally let go.' *Mother and Daughter* refers to the same emotions.

'The Warrior Dreams' series deals with the ultimate in 'letting go'; that of a mother who has nurtured and taken care of her son through his childhood years and then has to deal with the trauma of his going off to war. In most of this series the 'dreamer' is blindfolded.

The Warrior Dreams…His Mother Waits, 1987, was carved in soapstone and depicts a blindfold-ed young warrior; in his hand is a staff, denoting war, whilst the forefinger of his hand is resting apprehensively in his mouth. It is a powerful and moving sculpture that symbolises youth, inno-cence and vulnerability. His mother's face is carved on the reverse of the sculpture, and there is another emotional element which came out of the stone by chance, as Dawn explains

> As I was working on this sculpture there was a piece of stone at the top which I would nor-mally have just lopped off. Yet something inside me told me that I must not do this. At the time it wasn't apparent why I had to leave it there. Eventually I realised what it was for –

Mother and Daughter, 1991, soapstone, 61 x 38 x 21cms. Private Collection. Photo by M Hollow

Despair, 2000, bronze, 148 x 33 x 23cms. Photo by Nigel Hillier

it became the hand that joined the mother to her son.

This sculpture was also cast in bronze in 1996.

Other sculptures in the 'Warrior' series show the inevitable path of war. In *Fallen Warrior,* the boy, still blindfolded and still holding his staff, is seen mown down and in *The Final Dream* 1988, in Ancaster limestone, hands over his eyes like a blindfold, he prepares for death.

Many of Dawn's sculptures use double images; a subconscious development of her work, which, it has been suggested, is rooted in her twin status. Ultimately though, Dawn's interest in the nature of human interactions and those within families in particular, is at the foundation of these images. *My Sister...Myself* falls within the double-image category and was based on Dawn's magnificent Femme de Rocher series of 'knife-edge' sculptures, with sharply carved profiles that exude a strength and power associated with ancient sculptures. The contrast of rough and smooth textures and the subtle colours that come to light through the polished surface add various elements of interest. Both *Femme de Rocher* and *My Sister...Myself* were cast in bronze from the stone carving *Femme de Rocher. Sisters* 1994, carved in Ancaster Limestone, is another double-image sculpture, featuring two serene faces, one upright, the other horizontal, tenderly held together by a hand. Another carving produced in 2000 was also entitled *Sisters.* This was carved in Richemont limestone and shows two faces side by side. One is wearing a broad, textured blindfold over a beautifully smooth face, whilst the other is wide-eyed but has a face blemished with layers of braiding, like strips of plaster, pulled across her face. Each has a different set of advantages and disadvantages. They are the same, but different, and each is possibly dependent on the other. An example of 'The Family Unit' is portrayed in the sculpture *Embrace,* 2000. In this piece, which measures 143 cms high and is carved in Anstrude Clair Limestone, the family members are joined together by hands which encircle and weave through the sculpture.

Dawn's work is never purely ornamental; there is always a deep-rooted meaning in what she creates. *Never Again,* 1991, in Ancaster limestone, is another such example. Frustrated one day, Dawn screamed 'Never Again' and realised that those two words could apply to all kinds of situations. It has been the cry of people after atrocities like genocide and the holocaust. Dawn's own grandfather died in Auschwitz and she naturally feels particularly deep emotions about this atrocity.

An Emotional Year was carved from alabaster in 1995 during the year her father died. It shows four heads depicting the array of emotions Dawn felt during this difficult period when she would go to London to visit him in hospital and then come home and work on the sculpture. Dawn loves the beauty of alabaster, not the pure white variety, but the more highly

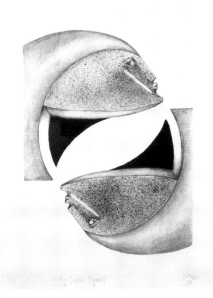

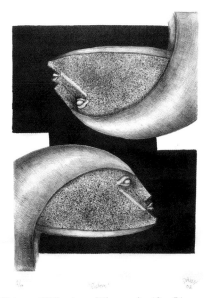

My Sister...Myself, 2002, stone lithograph,
68 x 56cms. Photo by Nigel Hillier

Sisters, 2002, stone lithograph, 68 x 56cms.
Photo by Nigel Hillier

My Sister...Myself, 2003, limestone, 62 x 112 x 42cms. Photo by Nigel Hillier

Embrace, 2000, Anstrude Clair limestone, 143 x 79 x 49cms

Sisters, 1994, Ancaster limestone, 33 x 56 x 28cms. Photo by Nigel Hillier

Sisters, 2000, Richemont limestone, 31 x 61 x 16cms. Photo by Matthew Hollow

coloured, earthy type with its amazing markings and translucency. She likes to use this delicate material to make strong statements and images. This sculpture was also cast in bronze.

Despair, 1982, carved from alabaster and cast in bronze in 2000, and *Fragile Emotions*, 1993, carved from soapstone, show the universal feeling of vulnerability when faced with difficult and demanding situations. The angular face of *Despair* has sharp contours that suggest introspection and suffering. *Fragile Emotions*, with the cracked relief on its surface, literally shows the cracking facade of a person no longer able to cope, but the hand is there again for protection and comfort.

Dawn sees family relationships as a complex affair; they can both nurture and destroy, heal and wound, give pleasure and create pain. *My Mother, Myself...My Daughter, Myself* carved in 1992 from alabaster, depicts the natural progression from a girl to womanhood and the relationship that ensues with each stage between mothers and daughters. The sculpted rope entwined around them, symbolically binds them together emotionally, and for generation after generation as the one becomes the other. Perhaps this is prophetic as Dawn's daughters are both artistic; Michelle went on to become an artist.

Dawn grasped the opportunity to use stone in a different way when, in 2003, she went with Malcolm on a three-month trip to Washington DC where she worked on a lithography series. In this technique, the stone is rubbed down with different grits of carborundum powder and sanded by hand with the help of a levigator (a steel plate with a handle) to produce the smoothest of surfaces. The image is then drawn directly onto the smoothed stone with special grease-based pens and inks so that the oil-based printing inks only adhere to the

Torso, 2000, charcoal on paper,
145 x 109cms. Private Collection

marks made by the pens. Under the pressure of the press, the image is printed onto paper. Wanting to use a familiar image while becoming accustomed to the process, Dawn used the 'Femme de Rocher' series on which to base the images for her exquisite stone lithographs.

In 2000, a meeting with Nicola Horlick, who made her name whilst working with Morgan Grenfell Asset Management, led to a huge and important commission for Dawn. Nicola's eldest daughter, Georgie, had died of leukaemia in 1998 when she was only twelve years old. Nicola wanted a sculpture as a lasting memorial and a celebration of Georgie's life. Having seen the emotional and sensitive qualities of Dawn's work at a gallery in London, Nicola realised that this would be the right person to produce the sculpture she wanted. Initially Dawn was unsure about accepting this commission because her work was generally about her own feelings and emotions. She felt this was different from most commissions as there would be a huge responsibility to capture Georgie in the way her family saw her, with their deep and very strong emotions being intrinsic to the sculpture. It was a daunting prospect to work on such a sensitive subject. She thought long and hard about it and eventually decided to accept the commission.

The two women looked at pictures of Georgie and began initial discussions about the vision for the sculpture. Dawn does not work in portrait sculpture, so it was decided that the finished work would be a representation of the essence of the child, as opposed to a true likeness; Nicola spoke of Georgie's constant smile and her beautiful hands and hair which 'was like sunshine.' Underlying this outer beauty, was an inner beauty, a kindness that shone through despite her ten years of illness and pain.

Displaying a huge amount of trust, Nicola accepted Dawn's desire that the piece should not be viewed until it was finished. During the early stage of carving Dawn has described being 'paralysed with worry about all of Nicola's feelings involved with the sculpture' and terrified of the weight of the responsibility before her. Following philosophical words from Malcolm she was encouraged to continue and finish the sculpture.

Nicola's visit to Dawn's studio to view the completed work was a highly charged meeting for both of them. Taking her time to walk around the piece, Nicola made no initial comments and Dawn was concerned that she found something disappointing about the sculpture. However, Dawn need not have worried as Nicola declared herself delighted with the work; the momentary hesitation was due to the carving of Georgie's cheeks that Dawn had depicted as full and round. Dawn could not have known that the effects of Georgie's medication had caused an accentuated fullness in Georgie's face. Using the photographs that she had of Georgie through all the stages of her childhood, Dawn had focussed on the fullness of the face as representing a young Georgie. Once Nicola saw the sculpture in this way too, she accepted Dawn's portrayal of her daughter.

Nicola had spoken of her desire that the stone sculpture should be a timeless piece in the tradition of ancient carvings, so that Georgie's presence would be with the family forever. Carved in creamy white Supai limestone from a quarry in Italy and completed in 2004, the three-tonne sculpture shows Georgie with her wonderful long hair, wound round her parent's hands at the back of the piece.

In a moving interview on 'Woman's Hour' on Radio Four Dawn and Nicola spoke of their own feelings about the sculpture; Nicola's comment, 'I knew I had the right sculptor' is surely a profound testament to both Dawn's empathy and her technical expertise.

The Silent Scream, 1992, alabaster, 46 x 16 x 16cms. Photo by Ian Tilton

*The Final Dream,*1988, Ancaster limestone, 56 x 21 x 26cms. Photo by Ian Tilton

The Final Dream (view 2)

Fragile Emotions, 1993, soapstone, 46 x 31 x 26cms. Photo by Matthew Hollow

LIVERPOOL JOHN MOORES UNIVERSITY
LEARNING SERVICES

Self-Portrait, 2006, oil on board

Gina Ward

In Gina Ward's painting, *Self Portrait*, she stands, sideways on, looking tentatively at the viewer. There is a sense of fragility and uncertainty in her stance, as if captured in an intimate and unguarded moment, and an apparent hesitation to fully confront the onlooker. Beautifully painted in subtle tones, she seems to dissolve into the background. A quiet, shy young woman who appears younger than her years, Gina has successfully captured her own personality within this painting.

Likewise, the drawings that Gina produces perfectly mirror her personality. They have an uncontrived, honest and spontaneous air about them; at first glance appearing childlike but on closer inspection they show a natural skill, executed with a degree of sophistication that is truly amazing.

She was born in 1973 and, as a young child, she derived pleasure from illustrating stories that she had written. It was 1993 before she embarked on an arts foundation course at Padgate College, in Warrington where she lived. Although she continued to enjoy illustrating stories and poems such as Dylan Thomas's *Under Milk Wood*, the course was to allow her a year of creative freedom by experimenting with a large range of media. During this time, she produced very large drawings, sometimes measuring six feet by three feet, at times using ink, and at other times using brightly coloured oil pastels. Her use of bright colour on a large scale was inspired by the work of Gillian Ayres (b.1930). It is quite difficult to imagine Gina Ward producing colourful drawings on this scale, as the work for which she has gained considerable success is, typically, either monochromatic or partly coloured, as if unfinished, and would usually be on a much smaller scale; the largest of her drawings included in exhibitions have measured no more than approximately 14 x 18ins (35 x 41cm).

In 1994 Gina went to Edinburgh College of Art, beginning a degree course in illustration. However, finding this course creatively restrictive, she switched from illustration to painting and drawing where she was encouraged by her tutors and introduced to new methods and materials. She was taught how to use oil paints and used this medium to paint life models, allowing turpentine to drip onto the oils to give random effects, enjoying the element of chance intrinsic to the process. She experimented with the use of ink, applying it with a stick instead of brush

Photo by Nathan Roberts

Albert Square,
2002, pencil,
charcoal and ink.
Private Collection

Bolton Market,
2002, charcoal.
Collection
Wendy J Levy

in order to make her work freer and looser, some of her work became more expressionistic depicting her subjective and emotional response to objects and places. Drawings were developed using strong gestural marks with oil bars and graphite sticks. During this time, she was greatly inspired by the Scottish artist, Joan Eardley (1921–1963), who studied at the Glasgow School of Art during the early 1940s and whose work was free and expressive, capturing the street life in Glasgow at that time, portraying people with a blend of realism and compassion but without any sense of sentimentality. Gina echoed this delicate balance in the drawings of her elderly subjects, observed frequenting the cafés or sitting on benches.

She enjoyed Edinburgh; steeped in history, it resonated with her own romantic soul. The old cobbled streets and majestic buildings provided her with a wealth of subject matter. Outdoor she used acrylics as well as pastels and ink. Never using photographs or sketches as reference, all her work was finished on the spot, directly from the subject. This proved to be a good discipline for Gina; having previously worked from imagination, she now found herself observing and drawing all that was around her.

During her final year, Gina's drawings and paintings had become smaller and more sensitive. She was satisfied that her work had developed and improved as a result of working directly from life and by this time she felt ready to exhibit her work. A joint student exhibition at the Royal Scottish Academy proved to be a turning point for Gina as she sold her first painting, a self-portrait, to one of the secretaries who worked there. The Academy was so enamoured of her work that they kept some of her paintings for their collection. The poet Michael Longley, father of one of Gina's friends, also became a fan of her work, purchasing several pieces from her degree show. Gina completed a successful degree course, being awarded First Class Honours.

She also won the John Kinross Scholarship which enabled her to go to Florence for three

Street, 1998, oil bar and pencil. Private Collection

Horse and Basil, 2005, oil on board. Private Collection

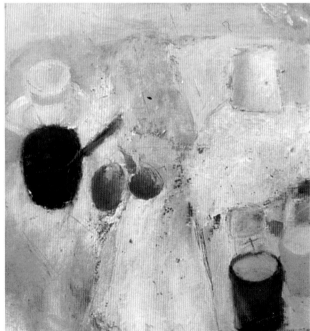

Tabletop, 1998, acrylic on board. Private Collection

*Cars And Bridges near
Deansgate*, 2005, mixed
media. Private Collection

Hebden Bridge, 2002, ink and
watercolour.
Collection Wendy J Levy

Liverpool Market, 2005, ink

Overlooking the Thames, 2003, charcoal and pencil

months following her degree. She travelled around Italy, marvelling at the crumbling old buildings and magical light of Siena. In Florence she drew the architecture and captured the activity of people congregating in the markets and sitting in parks. She spent many hours visiting the galleries and museums, being particularly attracted to the work of Botticelli (1445–1510), Canaletto (1697–1768) and Giotto (1267–1337).

On her return from Italy in 1999, Gina settled in Manchester and was offered studio space by Hilary Jack at Rogue Studios, Hanover Mill. Rogue had been established in 1995 by its founding members, David Gledhill, Judith Aitken, Colin Sinclair (d. 2005), Pete Jones (d. 2004) and Abraham Emajaro. Their former studio, 'Cuba', in Ancoats, had burned down, so they relocated in Hanover Mill, soon being joined by John Hamilton and Hilary Jack who took on a leading administrative role within the group. Hanover Mill housed a considerable artists' colony at that time, MASA – the Manchester Artists Studios Association – also rented space there.

Gina received a great deal of encouragement from the community of artists and a turning point came when Hilary Jack introduced Gina's work to the Wendy Levy Gallery in Didsbury. The drawings were accepted, some selling almost immediately. Gina visited the gallery a few days later to see her work hanging on the walls, but left without saying a word because she was too shy to introduce herself. Her work continued to arouse people's interest, not least her fellow artists. Those artists who have bought her work include Hilary Jack, Liam Spencer, David Hancock, Ian Jarman and John Blenkinsopp (who continues to collect Gina's drawings). She has also exchanged work with Sheila Meeks and other artists.

Living in Manchester, she was attracted by the changes that were taking place in the city, the juxtaposition of the old and new buildings and the lively atmosphere of her new surroundings. She produced her characteristic spidery and skilfully scribbled ink drawings of tiny figures dwarfed by the surrounding buildings of St Peter's Square. She made many drawings of Albert Square, as she did of the busy bars and arched bridges in the Deansgate area. Some of these drawings were enhanced with pastel, watercolour or charcoal, all drawn from life and completed on the spot.

Gina made trips to nearby towns for further inspiration. Finding the market place in Bolton, she drew the local women, carrying shopping bags and wearing headscarves, as they assembled around the market stalls like bees around a honeypot. The steep roads of Hebden Bridge where cottages cling tenuously to the hilly landscape provided good subject matter. Enthused by the uneven and vulnerable appearance of the houses, she would use an unusual perspective to exaggerate and successfully depict the atmosphere of this interesting town. Gina continues to enjoy drawing and painting, on the spot, in Liverpool, where her sister lives. Motivated by the wealth of architecture, the ambience of the docks and the character of the city, she has depicted many aspects of the place in all types of media. In Southport, Gina was not so much attracted by the houses and scenery but rather by the older residents. Old-fashioned seaside resorts seem to attract senior citizens and Gina delights in observing them, sitting on benches, looking out to sea.

Before moving to London with her partner, Nathan, in 2003, she shared an exhibition with John Pegg at the Wendy Levy Gallery, also showing her work with Comme Ça in the same year. An extremely successful solo show was to follow at the Wendy Levy Gallery two years later. During her year in London, Gina continued to work as a classroom support assistant for children with special needs. London was quite a daunting and awe-inspiring place for Gina. She kept her work quite simple, concentrating on making quick, lively drawings of her surroundings. The tiny sketch entitled *Looking at the Thames* was produced shortly after moving to the city and expresses the delight and romance of living in such a vast, vibrant and culturally thriving environment. She enjoyed working by the Thames, capturing life on the river against the backdrop of the famous landmark buildings.

Fog behind Victoria Station, 2005, mixed media.
Private Collection

Tenby, 2006, ink, oil pastel and pencil

During her time in London she recalls visiting an exhibition of paintings by Edouard Vuillard (1868–1940). Gina could easily relate to this intimate, domestic genre; his work was often small in scale, moody and rather mysterious. Gina's series of tiny 'Shoe' paintings are precious little pieces, intimate and sensitive, painted with a palette so delicate that it is almost a whisper, as if allowing the viewer a mere glimpse into the private world of the owner of the shoes. The same applies to her 'Horse' series, in which the little figure of a horse, an ornament belonging to Gina, is placed on a table, perhaps close to other personal belongings, or close to a plant, creating what is apparently a very personal still-life. Gina has always been impressed by the paintings of Gwen John (1876–1939), who achieved this same private and introspective quality in her muted paintings. Gina also admires the work of Edward Hopper (1882–1967), being much inspired by the Tate Modern's exhibition of his work which she visited whilst living in London.

At the end of 2004 Gina and Nathan moved to Penarth, a small seaside town near Cardiff, where Gina continues to work with autistic

Deansgate, 2001, pencil and ink. Private Collection

children. Gina feels much more at home in this beautiful, quiet area, away from the noise and crowds of large cities. In this environment she feels comfortable sitting outside to draw and paint. Penarth sits in a lovely hilly landscape with the bays of Cardiff close by. Once a busy dockland, Cardiff's terraces of dockers' cottages have attracted Gina's attention and she has produced many drawings and paintings of the area. She has also been exploring and finding new inspiration in various locations around Penarth. The nearby valley towns have provided her with inspiring material and she has captured their characteristic claustrophobic atmosphere in drawings such as *Penrhiwceiber*. The seaside town of Tenby has also attracted her attention with its clusters of colourful houses and large sweeping bay.

Although she delights in producing these exquisite drawings in her unique style, a desire to express herself in a more abstract way is beginning to stir inside her. She finds herself attracted to the work of the abstract expressionist Richard Diebenkorn (1922–1993), whose work often treads the delicate line between abstraction and figuration. Gina's current instinct is to extend the boundaries of her work, not only by revisiting abstract painting but also by producing work on a much larger scale as she had done at university. This poses daunting logistical problems as she will not contemplate any way of working other than directly from

St Peters Square, 2005, charcoal and pencil and oil pastel. Private Collection

the subject, wherever that might be. Taking a series of photographs or making preparatory sketches is not something that Gina would normally choose to do; she feels that this would compromise the spontaneity and freshness inherent in her work. She says, 'The passion I feel when seeing an interesting subject for the first time, would be lost.'

However, she is very gradually beginning to acknowledge that it may only be possible to complete large paintings in a studio. She is, therefore, looking towards a compromise; she wants to experiment with completing a drawing on the spot and then working it up to a painting in the studio. This is an idea she holds for the future and, if it comes to fruition, will be a mighty, considerable and exciting development.

Ghislaine Howard

Ghislaine Howard's powerful paintings portray the human body at its most vulnerable and emotional moments: birth, love, death and the journey towards inner understanding confront the viewer from her canvases. Brutally honest, open, loving and compassionate, they arise from the artist's relationship with the business of living.

Ghislaine Howard was born in Eccles in 1953. Her Irish-born mother, Maureen, had married Martin, an actor whom she met whilst nursing in Stratford-upon-Avon shortly after the war. Martin had grown up in a north-east mining village and had been immersed in music since his earliest years. Ghislaine was the second of five children. She was christened Ghislaine Marianne Dobson but as a child she was teased at school about the name Ghislaine and insisted that her family and friends used her second name, Marianne. It was only much later, when she began to exhibit as an artist that she reverted to the name she had come to prefer: Ghislaine. All her siblings were boys and whilst all five children inherited their father's interest in music she alone developed a passion for the visual arts.

Ghislaine's childhood home reflected her mother's flair for colour and contained an eclectic mix of images, Victorian paintings, contemporary prints, paintings by Martin and – of great importance to her development – three reproductions that she found magical. One was a print of an interior by Matisse, another a beach scene by Gauguin, but the most significant of all was a reproduction of a drawing by Van Gogh of an old man sitting by a fire with his head in his hands. Seeing this as a small child, she was often reduced to tears as she tried to imagine why the old man was so sad. Inspired by such works, Ghislaine remembers from her earliest years that what she most wanted was to put into her drawings of people and animals a sense of physicality, movement and feeling.

Another frame of artistic reference included the powerful, if somewhat theatrical, religious images she saw in church every Sunday. Ghislaine attended a strict convent school where the disciplined art classes gave her little chance for freedom of expression or experimentation. Her skills really developed during Saturday morning classes, run by Harold Riley in Salford, and through her own constant sketching of horses, dogs and

Photo by Michael Howard

Father and Child, 1984, oil on canvas,
82 x 58cms

Lovers, 2001, oil on canvas, 127 x 76cms

the people living nearby.

In 1971 Ghislaine attended an art foundation
course at Manchester Polytechnic. The experience was
a revelation. She was given all the freedom she needed
to explore the language of brushstrokes and the sensu-
ous qualities of oil paint. She learnt to draw from life
and was encouraged to explore the qualities of disciplined drawing and colouristic painting. Following her
foundation course in Manchester, Ghislaine continued
her studies in Fine Art at Newcastle University in 1972.
At first she embraced the new ways of working that she
encountered, finishing her first year as a prize-winning
student working on large abstract expressionist canvases. However, she felt that this was not enough to
sustain her and felt the old pull towards working with
the human form. Figurative work was, to some extent,
out of favour at the time, but undeterred by this, she
worked largely on her own in the life room producing
powerful paintings and drawings of figures which
incorporated self-portraiture and interpretations of
the monumental casts from classical antiquity which
lined the life room. Ghislaine was seeking to situate
herself in relation to the tradition of such artists as
Titian, Rembrandt, Delacroix, and Cézanne. Looking
to them for nourishment, she was seeking a means to
develop her passion for figurative paintings in such a
way that would convey a sense of energy and emotion.
In her small attic studio during her last year at university, she produced, as a major element of her final
exhibition, a large, dramatic painting of a naked figure
diving from a boat. The painting was inspired by two
sources of art: a small gouache painting of a diving figure by Cézanne, and a dramatic episode from the
novel *Women in Love* by DH Lawrence. Ghislaine

Pregnant Self-portrait, July 1984, oil on board, 80 x 57cms. Private Collection

remembers the painting as an ambitious precursor of her future work. Perhaps the most significant event of Ghislaine's time at Newcastle was her meeting her future husband, art historian and painter, Michael Howard. Michael's passion for art and literature has been a continual source of delight, support and inspiration to her.

On finishing University, Ghislaine left the northwest for London where she took on part-time work whilst continuing to develop her painting. She exhibited her work in several group shows including the Chelsea Artists Group. She spent some time in France and looked closely at the work of Bonnard, Vuillard and Cézanne. This inspired her to paint smaller scale work; intimate interiors with rich colouration depicting herself and her relationship with Michael, her friends and family.

She returned to Manchester in 1980 with Michael who had taken a position as a lecturer in art history at Manchester Polytechnic. They were married soon after. Her first exhibition in the region was at Monks Hall Museum in Eccles. It was a celebration of her new life. She also found the changing environment of Salford and Manchester a source of constant interest. Having lived there and been to school there, her emotional ties to the city lured her again to its streets and canals where she recorded the demolition and building work going on all around her.

A major turning point in Ghislaine's career came in 1984 when, pregnant with her first child, she began to draw her changing body, using thick sticks of scene painter's charcoal on a heavy, coarse-grained watercolour paper. This powerful technique allowed her to draw and re-draw, catching shifts of position and charting, in the process, the passage of time and changing emotional states. Always preferring to work from personal experience, Ghislaine had unselfconsciously charted the course of her pregnancy and in so doing, produced studies of this shared human condition. In *Study for Self Portrait*, July 1984 and in the subsequent painting of the same title we see Ghislaine seated. The weight of her body seems almost too much to bear; one arm rests on a table, her hand supporting her head; she is weary and passive, awaiting a life experience over which she has no control. Her eyes are unclear and averted; she does not gaze directly at the viewer, giving a strong impression that she is wrapped up in her own thoughts. The form itself is self-contained within dark, heavy strokes and the dark bands of colour at the top and left-hand side of the picture further emphasise this self-absorption of the figure. She is at once cocooned and isolated – pregnancy may be a shared human condition, but each woman's experience of it is utterly personal.

Once her son, Max, was born, Ghislaine had no need to look further for her subject matter. She worked furiously, in her studio at home, often with the baby in a sling across her body, to produce work for an imminent exhibition at Salford Art Gallery. Turning from a depiction of the single figure, Ghislaine now rejoiced in painting her family. Work periods had to be very focused, and with limited time and enforced concentration, she captured those intimate moments of family life when two become three. We see her gazing adoringly down at her baby as he feeds; there is little separation of the two forms which are contained within a suffused glow. We also see *Michael with Max* sharing a moment of delight with the baby being swung high into the air and squealing with joy.

Mother Embracing Her Child was painted in 1985 after Ghislaine had glimpsed a mirror image of herself hugging Max, in the studio. Using a series of preliminary drawings, the final oil painting on canvas is a universal image of mother and child. Ghislaine cradles Max in her arms, her head slightly forward to kiss the side of his face; her baby's arms and legs wrap around her. There is a strong sense of physical movement in the painting – this is not a passive embrace but one of fierce intensity. Ghislaine's face is hidden behind Max's half turned head as he pulls away from his mother's perhaps too sudden show of affection. The initial drawing for *Self-Portrait*, July 1984 was placed in the background to suggest the passage of time.

Having felt blessed and nourished by her family and rejoicing in her baby's first months, Ghislaine began to feel acutely aware of the other end of life's spectrum. The birth of Max had awakened in her a profound sense of her own mortality and an almost unbearable awareness of the fragility of human life with its inevitable cycle of birth and death. Ghislaine and her family had made their home in an old tripe works in the centre of the Derbyshire town of Glossop, close to the open moors of the Peak District National Park. She began to make regular visits to the residents of the geriatric unit at the town's Shire Hill Hospital. At the hospital, she was able to chart the details of their everyday lives with the care and compassion that underpins all her work. A moving moment came when, just at the time Max was learning to walk, she watched the painful progress of an old lady learning to walk again after suffering a stroke.

With the birth of her daughter, Cordelia, in 1987, Ghislaine continued to record those precious moments of family life that strengthen and define any family unit. In the painting *Cordelia in the Green Kitchen*, 1994, Ghislaine portrays the young Cordelia concentrating on her meal. The atmosphere is quiet and tranquil. A bright bowl of fruit in vibrant yellows and rich warm ochres sits on a blue/green table and Cordelia is dressed in darker tones of blue. The green walls and cheerful curtains at the window continue the unity of colouration through the picture.

In 1991 Ghislaine approached Manchester Art Gallery with the idea of mounting an

Michael with Max, 2004, oil on canvas,
145 x 100cms

Feeding Max, 1984, oil on canvas,
176 x 120cms

*Cordelia in the
Green Kitchen*,
1995,
oil on canvas,
90 x 90cms

Midwife Waiting to Receive the New Child, 1993, oil on canvas, 120 x 76cms

Birth Painting, oil on canvas, 120 x 156cms

exhibition of paintings on the theme depicting the journey of life from birth to death. Two years later, part of her idea came to fruition when Manchester Art Gallery commissioned a four-month residency at St Mary's Hospital Maternity Unity to produce a series of works relating to childbirth. This presented Ghislaine with a unique challenge.

She writes in her journal on the first day of the residency

My daughter was born here five years ago, so I arrive for my first day as artist-in-residence with mixed feelings of familiarity and displacement. There is the same walk to the doors of the ante-natal clinic, the same queue of women waiting. The maternity unit is an extraordinary institution: it is here the experience takes place that we have all shared – our naked entry into the world.

I talk to some women in the corridor waiting to be seen by doctors, but these initial approaches are very difficult. If I am to work with any patient she must sign a consent form, which instantly formalises everything but is a necessary legal precaution. Most women immediately anticipate an invasion of their privacy and look away.

I approach a young woman and her partner. She smiles, so I sit down and explain who I am. It is her first visit and she agrees to allow me through with her. She is nervous and her English is not very good. The doctor is pleasant but brisk – not an easy atmosphere; I must learn to make relationships with both sides. A few rapid drawings of the examination result. This first contact reveals in a very clear way the scale of the task ahead.

Depicting events before, during and after birth, this body of work is monumental in its frankness and its total empathy. These sketches and paintings are not simply the practised observations of the artist's eye; they speak to us of our vulnerability and powerlessness; but they also speak of our triumph over adversity. So we see antenatal examinations where the expectant mother lies passive, exposing her huge belly to probing hands. She is in an ambiguous state; neither ill in the sense of a patient requiring treatment, nor feeling in control of her body which needs monitoring.

In the painting *Couple during Labour*, we see the pair, arms entwined. The viewer empathises with both the male and female figures. The man offers comfort and puts a strong arm around the woman; we can't see their expressions but we understand the gestures, one arm clinging, the other one protective. The female figure almost fills the canvas and we can feel the pain in her twisted shape. She is the main player in the story; the male has to play the supportive role and we see him almost as a shadowy figure, his body powerless in this huge event.

The main event, the birth, is graphically and uncompromisingly depicted in a series of drawings and paintings. A rush of activity now replaces the enforced waiting of the labour period. In the *Birth Painting*, the woman's body has become public property exposed in all its intimate detail; all sense of privacy has gone. Disconnected arms and hands probe within; they are competent, professional hands that have performed these tasks many times before. Ghislaine portrays these hands as both strong and gentle as the new baby is delivered.

Having witnessed the Caesarian birth of twins, Ghislaine produced a painting that contrasts with the relative normality and excited anticipation in the delivery room. This painting depicts the clinical atmosphere of the operating theatre. Wanting to portray the birth from the mother's viewpoint, Ghislaine stood by the woman's head to draw the scene of the first baby being brought out and lifted into the light.

Executed in vigorous bold strokes of oil on canvas, this series of paintings invites the viewer to share at close quarters the mystery, pain and wonder of these extraordinary yet everyday moments. The fine detail of a scene is sacrificed for atmosphere and movement. Although facial features are often indistinct, the subject matter is always examined closely, giving a sense of drama, involvement and immediacy. In art as in life, Ghislaine is not a dispassionate or distant onlooker.

Despite her initial apprehension when she embarked on this courageous project,

Ghislaine felt compelled to complete this series of paintings. The resulting exhibition, 'A Shared Experience', was shown at Manchester City Art Gallery in 1993 and at the Wellcome Foundation in London in 1994. Some of the paintings also formed part of a show, 'Beginnings and Endings', an exhibition of paintings and drawings depicting birth and death, at the Whitworth Art Gallery in 1999.

The innovative nature of this body of work should not be underestimated. Very rarely depicted in western art and then usually from a romanticised, religious or male perspective, the pregnant and delivering figures have rarely been shown with such intimacy and honesty.

Having worked within such a particular institution as St Mary's Hospital, with its covert and overt sets of rules and codes of behaviour, Ghislaine set out to witness life at a very different institution. In her desire to continue to feel, understand and convey the human condition, she embarked on an art project at Risley Prison. At the end of 1993 she spent two weeks conducting art workshops with a group of twelve male inmates and then spent several weeks producing her own studies of different aspects of life there. The work that resulted from this unique collaboration was shown at an exhibition, 'Inside Out' at Warrington Art Gallery.

These paintings and drawings capture the routines of everyday prison life and give a sense of the underlying tensions and intense relationships that underpin the often tedious regime that is prison life. One particularly harrowing painting, *Seg Unit*, 1994, shows an inmate, segregated in a special cell after attempting suicide. Painted in different shades of grey and blue, it portrays an almost unbearably claustrophobic atmosphere. The cell is bare but for a cardboard chair and the mattress where the man is seen, huddled under a blanket like a tortured animal, his face peering from behind the covers, his eyes expressionless.

In 1994 Manchester was designated the Arts Council's City of Drama and Ghislaine embarked on a project to work with a number of theatres to portray the actors' world. A place of heightened emotion and dramatic intensity, the theatre is, in some respects, not unlike a hospital or prison; the participants in all these scenarios are brought together temporarily and create artificial but very close personal relationships, before moving apart again to resume their normal lives. In the dressing rooms and during readings and rehearsals, Ghislaine documented the energy of the actors as they explored and developed their roles.

As a very necessary balance to the dramatic and emotionally intense work that Ghislaine has created, she has also worked on many joyful pieces. She has always painted as a matter of course landscapes and domestic scenes which are important elements of her art, nourishing and sustaining her more public works. Through friends and acquaintances she found herself often in the company of dancers: a subject close to the heart of one of her greatest heroes,

Leaving the Ward, 2004, acrylic on canvas, 102 x 128cms

Edgar Degas. This has led to a number of exciting projects, such as film work where she and her husband worked together to help reconstruct not only Degas' paintings, prints and sculpture, but also his studio and all its paraphernalia.

Like Bonnard or Vuillard, Ghislaine's everyday life has remained at the centre of her working practice. A painting that embodies this is a wonderful study of herself and Cordelia, both naked, standing side by side looking intently into a mirror. In this painting, Ghislaine fulfills the need most parents have – to capture a precious time in life, a time that may be forgotten too soon with the passing years.

Similarly, Ghislaine produced a painting of Michael and herself sharing an intimate embrace. With his hand tenderly cradling the back of her head the painting evokes an atmosphere of shared affection and concern. Some of her paintings were exhibited at the 'Intimacy' show, a group exhibition at the Lowry art gallery in 2002, and are a testament to Ghislaine's profound belief in the nurturing relationships that may be found in family life.

Latterly Ghislaine has been inspired to produce a delightfully poignant series of very small paintings of clothes. These celebrate the personalities that clothes take on through use. They explore the traces of the past that cling onto clothes now too small, too old fashioned or simply too worn out for use. These themes have become particularly poignant as her children have grown into adulthood, during which process she has captured on canvas the moments of development of both her son, Max, a singer and writer of songs and stories, and her daughter, Cordelia, an actress, musician and artist, both of whom continue to feed and nourish Ghislaine's creative life.

Since her time at St Mary's Hospital Maternity Unit, Ghislaine found herself thinking once again of the religious themes and images from her childhood. In the labour wards, she had been witness to many scenes that brought to mind images from the New Testament and with these visions in mind she embarked upon a body of work, 'Stations of the Cross/The Captive Figure', that was to fully occupy her for the next few years.

Although based on a religious theme, the work is essentially a profound comment on man's inhumanity to man. While portraying the pain of Christ, the paintings deal with the universality of pain and with the experience of all who have suffered and continue to suffer miscarriages of justice at the hands of others. With access to a good model, Ghislaine worked with him as he acted out the sequence of events associated with Christ's journey to Calvary. They developed together a sequence of poses to represent a specific moment in the

Mother and Daughter, 1984, acrylic on canvas, 128 x 102cms

The Embrace, 1987, acrylic on canvas, 128 x 102cms

The Lamentation of the Women of Jerusalem,
1999, acrylic on canvas, 183 x 142cms

narrative, each one of which has become a universal image – as relevant today as it was two thousand years ago. Thus we see Christ on the journey from condemnation to death; each image in sombre, monochromatic tones of blacks, greys and whites. He is a lone figure, bearing his fate with stoical courage, but at some points along the journey he is given help by compassionate bystanders. Simon of Cyrene shares the suffering and helps bear the cross; further along the road, Veronica wipes his face, an image developed by Ghislaine from an earlier painting of a midwife waiting to receive the new child with a cloth. In *Lamentation of the Women of Jerusalem*, Ghislaine portrays two women, overcome with grief, comforting each other. They are huddled together, the younger one pregnant, seeming to support the older woman. They present a united empathetic and iconic image signifying their compassion with Christ's suffering. A drawing for this painting was presented to the Queen for the Royal Collection when Ghislaine's work was exhibited at Gloucester cathedral in 2004.

Like all powerful religious paintings, the sequence 'Stations of the Cross/The Captive Figure' is rooted in human experience. Ghislaine's work speaks to the religious and non-religious in a universal language of suffering, vulnerability, compassion and humanity.

As part of Liverpool Hope University College's millennium project, and supported by Amnesty International, the subsequent exhibition of these fourteen powerful paintings was shown at Liverpool's Anglican and Roman Catholic Cathedrals in 2000. Since then the sequence has been seen in many interesting and diverse venues, returning to be exhibited at Liverpool from time to time.

Recognition of Ghislaine's achievement in the area of painting has taken many forms, for example, a twenty-five foot high altarpiece for Liverpool Hope University College, and in 2004 she participated in an exhibition at St Paul's Cathedral in London where her work was shown in the company of Bill Viola, Tracey Emin and other notable contemporary artists.

Funeral, 2005, acrylic on canvas,
152 x 122cms

Three Women at a Funeral, 2004, acrylic on
canvas, 91 x 91cms

Other major commissions have followed.

But, with the death of her father in 2004, Ghislaine turned again to her own experiences and recorded her bereavement in a series of powerful paintings. One such painting captures a poignant moment with her father lying ill in a hospital bed and her mother bending down to hug him in a moving embrace. She is dressed in lilac, her husband's favourite colour.

In a painting depicting a moment at her father's funeral, Ghislaine portrays the inner strength of her mother. Dressed in dark tones, she is painted with her back to us, with her arms around two women who had helped look after her husband. It is an emotional painting depicting pain, support and nurture. A further painting of the interment shows the three generations of women all lost in their own thoughts. Cordelia, bearing flowers, stands with her mother and grandmother. Ghislaine appears to be looking at her daughter and mother in a protective gesture, absorbing their emotions as well as her own. Ghislaine has been inspired by her mother's strength in dealing with her loss. Despite a debilitating illness she has continued to live her life with great energy, developing her writing and discovering her own very personal gift for painting.

Ghislaine has never been concerned about working against the tide of fashion. For her the important thing to attempt is to communicate, in a clear and accessible way, something of the huge issues that define us as human beings. She is unafraid of confronting her responses to intimate personal experiences which, to differing degrees, we all share. Here is an artist who will continue to pay homage to life itself in her powerful and thought-provoking paintings.

Light into Shadow, 1988, watercolour, 56 x 76cms. Private Collection

Islands and Light, 1996, watercolour, 56 x 74cms. Private Collection

Jenny Ryrie

'I am drawn by the special properties of fluidity and translucency of water-based media on a white ground; the layers of depth when washes overlap, the subtle richness of the watercolour palette.' These are the words of Jenny Ryrie who, metaphorically speaking, has watercolour running through her veins. Her father's ancestors produced four successive generations of watercolour artists from 1762–1949 who all taught art at Eton College, and included William Evans of Eton (1798–1877). It comes as no surprise, therefore, that Jenny Ryrie is a watercolourist.

She was born, Jennifer Ann Whitcombe, in 1957 in Lincolnshire. When she was a small child the family moved to Leamington Spa, Warwickshire, and when she was seven years old, to Cheshire. Always known as Jenny, she was the youngest of three siblings and was the only one to have inherited the artistic gene. Because of the artistic thread running through her family, Jenny was always encouraged to paint.

Since childhood she has been interested in all aspects of nature and natural forms. Her love of horses has emerged as a recurrent theme: horses in forests, reminiscent of days spent riding bareback in Delamere Forest, winding between the pine trees.

There have been, broadly, three aspects to her painting career: firstly, her early landscapes that became slightly abstracted and increasingly fluid, conveying an intense use of light and simplified forms; then her paintings of America, in particular the exploration of symbols within the landscape and its underlying energies and mysticism; and thirdly, since 2000, the emergence of total abstraction, exploring pure sensation, partly triggered by listening to music. It has been a fruitful journey for Jenny Ryrie and has taken her a long way since she first picked up her paintbrushes.

After leaving school in Chester in 1975, she embarked on an M.A. in Fine Art, a course that consisted of five years study at the Edinburgh College of Art and Edinburgh University, specialising in drawing and painting. Some of the leading Scottish artists of the day were lecturers during Jenny's time there, including Elizabeth Blackadder (b.1931), David Michie (b.1928) and Sir Robin Philipson (1916–1992) who was Head of Edinburgh College of Art and the President of the Royal Scottish Academy.

Photo by David Heke

After graduating she began to sell her paintings through exhibitions and the Edinburgh Fringe. From 1981 to 1985 she worked on commissions for botanical illustrations. Her first project was acquired through her brother's research in the Sultanate of Oman, with the University of Durham; it involved close inspection of insects and plants in order to produce watercolour illustrations that had to be scientifically accurate for their reproduction in a book, *Honey Bees in Oman*. The study of these botanical and zoological subjects has fed into later paintings of landscapes with isolated shapes of unusual plant forms, butterflies and birds. Her enjoyment of nature and wildlife, and the research for the book illustrations had led to an association with the Royal Botanic Gardens in Edinburgh where she was taught how to use electron microscopes to look at plant specimens. This led to further commissions to produce black-and-white botanical illustrations which, in turn, led to a commission for watercolour illustrations of British wild flowers for the Department of Zoology at Cardiff University.

By this time, Jenny was living in South Wales, having moved there in 1984 with her husband, Neil Ryrie, whom she had married in 1978. Her work was beginning to loosen up, and, living in the Cynon Valley near Brecon National Park, was inspired by the scenic landscape and a growing interest in waterfalls followed. Her first real breakthrough in subject-matter came in 1985 when she discovered the beautiful waterfalls in the Vale of Neath. Recalling the moment she says, 'In particular, Sgwd yr Eire is a lovely waterfall that you can walk right behind on the old sheep drovers' track. Standing on the rocks looking straight through the veils of white water pouring down in front of you is an amazing primal experience, especially when bright sunlight transforms the falls into a glittering curtain of light. All the senses are stimulated at once, with the roaring thunder of the water, the smell of damp rock and vegetation and the feel of cool spray against your skin. I had the same experience in Switzerland, walking behind the Giesbach Falls near Interlaken, which I have also painted several times.' This arousing of the senses, experienced through the waterfalls, led to a desire to convey the sensation of light and sound in a more abstract way.

In 1986, while Jenny was still in South Wales, Ella was born. At that time Jenny was beginning to exhibit and sell her work in Chester. By 1987, Jenny and Neil had separated and she moved back to Chester with Ella. She had her first solo exhibition in 1988, mainly semi-abstract paintings of waterfalls, at the Ayling Porteous Gallery in Chester. Included in the exhibition were various paintings of Liverpool; the cathedrals and the Liver Buildings had been inspirational subjects. The paintings sold very well and in the same year she shared an exhibition with two other women artists at the Lamont Gallery in London. She was a single mum, living in a small house in Chester and needing time to devote to her career in order to support her small child. As if heaven sent, she met two other mothers; one a singer, the other a singer and writer. They each needed time to work, so they took it in turn to look after each other's children. This enabled Jenny to give private lessons in watercolour painting whilst developing her career.

Propelled by a compulsion to explore the energies of the landscape through varying degrees of abstraction, Jenny gained inspiration from the many artists whose work she revered. Early influences were the German American artist Lyonel Feininger (1871–1956), and Russian Rayonism which was introduced to the public in 1913 and lasted only a year, but was a vital movement in the development of Russian abstract art. Jenny says, 'I liked the way the Rayonists created a composition by refracting the light from forms into a prismatic web of colours and tones.' She has been interested in many watercolourists, particularly American artists, for their strength of colour and tone as well as their mastery of technique: the virtuosity of John Singer Sargent (1856–1925) and Winslow Homer (1836–1910). Also the rich luminosity of the German Expressionist Emil Nolde (1867–1956), and the fluidity of the British artist William Tillyer (b. 1938). She likes the American Abstract Expressionists Robert Motherwell (1915–1991) and Jackson Pollock (1912–1956) for their breaking through to an almost cosmic level of abstraction. She also enjoys the work of Wassily Kandinsky (1866–1944) and Paul Klee (1879–1940) for their exploration of the lyrical and links between painting and music, a subject that is close to Jenny's heart. She particularly admires the imaginative and spiritual abstracts painted by Joan Miro (1893–1983) and enjoys his use of forms in space. Stimulated by the work of these inspired artists, Jenny's vision was related through her recurrent themes of deserts, plant forms and the sea, and the use of symbols which she poetically explains: 'Symbols indicate the mystical dimensions within the natural world and the omnipresence of powerful creative forces. Suns, circles and spirals represent light, water and life, while horses are symbols of beneficence, and birds are metaphors for the bridge between physical and spiritual states.' She worked in watercolour, sometimes introducing other materials such as acrylics and pastels to add opacity and texture to areas within the paintings. She also experimented with scale and began working on unusually large sizes of paper which had to be laid flat on the floor during the painting process.

The Thackeray Gallery, in London, started to exhibit her work in 1990; this led to a joint exhibition there in 1993 with Hans Schwarz (1922–2003). 1990 provided another turning point in Jenny's life when she married Philip Brockley, a geologist, with whom she explored America, making frequent visits over a number of years. She was inspired by the colours, scale

The Riotous Stars, 1998, watercolour and mixed media, 56 x 76cms. Private Collection

The Wheel of Harvest, 2006, watercolour, 38 x 53cms. Private Collection

Corn Guardians, 2006, watercolour and mixed media, 54 x 74cms. Private Collection

Jazz Nights, 2005, watercolour, 54 x 76cms. Private Collection

and variety of the vast tracks of wilderness – mountains, forests, plains and deserts.

> New Mexico is very special to me; the way the light creates haloes around plant forms such as the cholla cactus; the endless hills dotted with piñon and juniper trees; the horses grazing quietly beneath cottonwood trees; ancient petroglyphs (rock carvings) glimmering on rocky cliffs in the moonlight; the colours at sunset suffusing the mountains in watermelon pinks and reds. New Mexico is a mystical place where the landscape feels alive with its own magical presence.

Relishing the new subject matter, she experimented with intense colour and form; creating large, semi-abstract landscapes of Arizona and New Mexico.

Her introduction to New Mexico came about through Phil's work in the oil industry and his American contacts. They researched many American galleries together and Jenny's work was accepted by Canyon Road Contemporary Art, a gallery in the centre of Santa Fe's vibrant art district, where she had solo exhibitions for six consecutive years. At the same time she was exhibiting with the Kingfisher Gallery in Edinburgh.

Although Jenny has enjoyed travelling around America, she is still drawn to the British coast, especially Cornwall with its golden light and pale turquoise sea, driftwood and shell forms. She also explored the wild scenery of Scotland, Wales and the Lake District, all of which have appeared in Jenny's paintings: 'I am also deeply moved by the more subtle pastoral landscapes of bleached stubble-fields, harvest moons and mysterious woods.'

In the early 1990s Jenny became involved in the Chester Fringe and became responsible for the exhibition programme. She co-ordinated artists and found venues where they could show their work. Through her endeavours and activities she came to know many Cheshire artists. She realised there was a wealth of talented people who generally work alone in their studios and who would benefit, professionally and socially, from having a network of like-minded people. Jenny suggested forming a group of Cheshire artists to meet on a regular basis to exchange ideas and information. The group thrived and was renamed 'P.A.C.' (Professional Artists in Cheshire). The members doubled in number and held many prestigious exhibitions. They took a stand at the 2002 Fresh Art Fair at the Business Design Centre in Islington. Jenny recalls the experience:

> It involved a small group of us staying in London for the week of the Fair during a July heat wave with a tube strike causing chaos, especially as our accommodation was miles from the Centre. We lost each other in the fight for buses, we acquired helpers and hangers-on, all wanting to stay at the same small house, much to the surprise of our long-suffering hostess, a cousin of mine, and we lost people to Rastafarian parties

as we returned, in the small hours, to Brixton where we were staying.

And a good time was had by all! For several years Jenny devoted a lot of time and hard work to the organisation of the co-operative. This successful network was something she is proud to have instigated and organised. In 2004 P.A.C. was amalgamated, for funding purposes, with Cheshire Open Studios and given a new name: C.A.N. (Cheshire Artists Network). It continues to evolve with a different membership and is now run by a committee.

As well as setting up P.A.C., Jenny has been involved with the organisation of exchange exhibitions in Europe through Chester's twinning programme. This has taken her to France, Italy and Germany in her endeavours to help promote the arts.

Music is another stimulating art form and inspires much of Jenny's current work. She plays the guitar and enjoys listening to all kinds of live music. Since 2002 the level of abstraction has steadily increased, and the total abstraction now achieved was initially inspired by listening to music. Jenny says, 'I wanted to create paintings that communicate through sensations of colour and form, without a visual reference point, in much the same way that music can evoke emotion through sounds without words.' This led to a series of paintings that relate specifically to music and Jenny calls 'lyrical abstracts.' Some evoke an overall mood – for example, orchestral or jazz, such as *Jazz Nights* – others concentrate on specific sounds of particular musical instruments, for example, *Rhythm and Splash,* which refers to the snare drums and 'splash' cymbals, conjuring up swishing metallic rhythms. These paintings explore the links between visual and aural sensations; at the simplest level darker tones and colours relate to deep sounds, bright acidic colours relate to high or shrill sounds. However, Jenny has developed a sophisticated vocabulary in paint to communicate sensations of sounds, rhythms, musical composition and the associated emotional response. She finds the watercolour medium ideal to achieve the full pictorial range, with broad saturated washes, intense linear brushwork, translucent veils of thin colour and 'spatter and drip' effects. In the summer of 2005 the C2 Gallery in Stoke Hammond, Buckinghamshire, arranged with the BBC for an exhibition of Jenny's abstract 'music' paintings to be on show at the Mermaid Theatre in London for the evening of the BBC Radio Jazz Awards ceremony. The exhibition consisted of twenty pieces of work and included the painting *Rhythm and Splash.* The event was compèred by Paul Gambaccini and saw performances by many leading jazz musicians such as Oscar Peterson.

Jenny has learned to predict and facilitate the wealth of 'watercolour accidents' that can be used to create subtle effects, such as feathering, blooms and backruns. The lyrical abstracts were further developed to explore sensations, not just of music, but an overlap of all the senses, such as movement and dance, or taste, smell and sound, as in *Tropical Symphony*. Hers

Poppy Encounter, 2006, watercolour, 38 x 53cms. Private Collection

Rhythm and Splash, 2005, watercolour, 54 x 74cms. Private Collection
Tropical Symphony, 2005, watercolour, 66 x 89cms. Private Collection

LIVERPOOL JOHN MOORES UNIVERSITY
LEARNING SERVICES

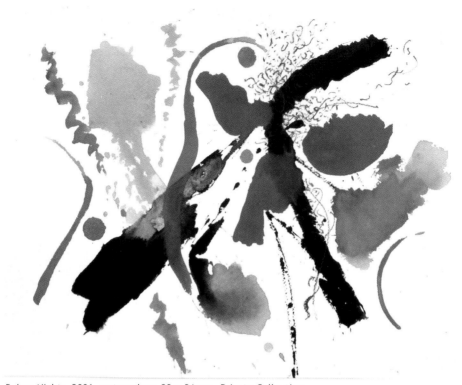

Bebop Nights, 2006, watercolour, 23 x 31cms. Private Collection

is not a conventional use of watercolour but explores and uses it to its limits.

In Jenny's latest paintings, such as *Poppy Encounter*, she revisits natural forms but in a pure abstract way. She has an insatiable appetite to encompass all aspects of watercolour painting, from detailed representation to the simplest suggestion; while some of her paintings retain visual references and are a response to nature and landscape, others are intense expressions of internal states of mind and the senses. Her work is evolving and revolving like the circular symbols in her paintings, and is as essential to her as that which those symbols represent: light, water and life.

Debbie Goldsmith

Debbie Goldsmith describes her work as 'intuitive, spontaneous and optimistic'. She was born in 1969 in Manchester and spent her formative years here. However, her main influences in art have been the abstract expressionists who developed a style of painting in America during the 1940s and 1950s. Abstract expressionism presents a broad range of stylistic diversity within its largely non-representational framework. For example, the expressive qualities of Willem De Kooning (1904–1997) or Helen Frankenthaler (b. 1928) are delivered in a completely different way from the images of Mark Rothko (1903–1970) who worked with simple, unified blocks of colour. Their stylistic differences, however, converge in their attention to surface qualities and it is this aspect that Debbie captures in her paintings. Working on large canvases, she places a good deal of importance on the texture of her paintings. She says, 'I am less concerned that the pieces appear representational and more concerned with the act of painting, making marks and gestures and putting colour together.'

Debbie's attraction to this style of art developed during her foundation course at Salford University where she enjoyed the help and encouragement she received from her tutors, Philip Aird, John Nuttall and Tim Dunbar. Debbie was given plenty of scope to experiment both with different styles and different materials. A quirk of circumstances meant that the art course was housed in an empty primary school where she had a huge room in which to work on her own. Having concentrated on life drawing at school and having always drawn figures as a child, she started to look at different ways of portraying the human form. She experimented by chopping up the form to make the drawing more abstract and expressionistic. Her sense of adventure in painting flourished and she enjoyed working with both figurative and abstract forms. As for many artists, her foundation course proved to be an enjoyable and informative time in which she began to discover herself as an artist.

The foundation course in Salford was followed by a BA Honours Degree in Fine Art at Coventry University. Debbie found the course at Coventry more intense and difficult than she had experienced in Salford. She describes her time at university:

> I was making large abstract paintings instinctively, not fully realising at the time why I was working in that way; that was the difficult thing, it was only much later, on reflection, that I

Photo by Mark Winkley

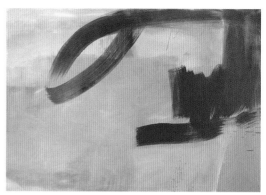

Loop, 1993, oil on canvas, 152 x 182cms

Slots, 2000, acrylic and pastel on paper,
91 x 60cms

understood where I was coming from. It was an intense time, your emotions run high being away from home and your friends, and for the first time being solely focused on making art. We would be encouraged to work for long periods of time and for most of that time left to our own devices. Looking back it wasn't an easy time for me but it was obviously an essential time that has driven the way I work today.

For her degree show Debbie experimented in producing pieces of work that emulated the style of the abstract expressionists where paint was thrown or dripped onto the canvas and left to flow in its own way. She was excited by the positive response to her work and by the fact that people were expressing an interest in collecting it. Several pieces were bought from the show by collectors both in the UK and abroad including a member of the 1980s band UB40.

Debbie left university in 1991 and returned to her Manchester roots, almost immediately taking a studio in Salford. There were only two or three other artists using the studio at the time. This presented a sharp contrast between the artistic environment at university, where she had been surrounded constantly by people who were either painting or talking about art,

Casino Drawing, 2000, acrylic and pastel,
121 x 91cms. Collection of the Lowry Hotel

Dancer, 2001, acrylic and pastel on canvas,
121 x 91cms. Private Collection

Traffic, 2000, oil and pastel on canvas,
154 x 121cms. Private Collection

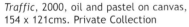

Wish You Were Where? 2001, Debbie Goldsmith and
Hilary Jack, suitcases, labels and wood, approx.
300 x 300cms. Collection of Manchester Art Gallery

and the loneliness she began to feel at the studio in Salford. After only a few months Debbie left the studio, fearing that she was becoming isolated from a broader artistic environment.

A short time later she was accepted by the Manchester Artists Studio Association (known as MASA), a group that was formed in 1983 by a number of graduates from Manchester Polytechnic. She joined the group during their move from their studios on Granby Row to new premises at Hanover Mill. Joining MASA at this time, during their move, gave Debbie the opportunity to get to know the other artists well as they all worked closely together as a team whilst building their studios within Hanover Mill. She found this an enjoyable and exciting time, working alongside a large group of artists who were already established members of MASA; artists such as Ben Cook, Liam Spencer, Alan Birch, Mark Bradley, Sheila Meeks, Martin Murrey, Michelle Leigh, Bill Longshaw, Paul Cordwell and Sue Platt. With a large studio space and plenty of enthusiasm, Debbie immersed herself in the burgeoning Manchester art scene.

Having persuaded her foundation course tutor from Salford University to find her a part-time job when a position became available, Debbie began teaching art on a part-time basis to help finance her career as an artist. She taught fine art, visual studies and life drawing to foundation and GNVQ-level students at Salford University and Stockport College, while at the same time increasing her network within the art world.

During this period Debbie developed her association with the Castlefield Gallery which was founded by MASA in 1984. She worked there as a volunteer for several years before becoming a member of the committee, which led to her travelling around the country meeting eminent artists such as Bridget Riley (b. 1931) and Basil Beattie (b. 1935) whose work was exhibited at the gallery.

Her first solo exhibition was curated by Tim Dunbar and Janice Webster in 1993 at the Chapman Gallery, part of Salford University. The exhibition included paintings and drawings that were produced following trips to visit family in Oregon, USA. In the painting *Loop*, she recreated the sensations of travelling by air across a vast landscape with everything laid out below in a patchwork of different colours and textures, depicting the meeting of land and sea. Inspired by Rothko and De Kooning, Debbie used huge brushstrokes and dramatic marks to convey her sense of the world below.

Although Debbie admired the huge paintings that artists such as Rothko created, she wanted to explore the creation of smaller work. To this end, she started taking a sketchbook on her travels with the intention of returning to her first love, figure drawing, which she firmly believes gave her the technical discipline on which her creativity is based. There followed a development in her work with the return of figures and recognisable shapes, thus forming a bridge between abstract and figurative work. Not wanting to lose the element of abstraction, which is the main focus of her work, she began developing her own vibrant style where figures and abstraction are perfectly juxtaposed.

During 1997 Debbie visited New York where, from initial sketches, she produced a series of very abstract paintings, pared down to the bare minimum number of lines needed to explain her vision. Continuing to visit the USA during 1998 and 1999 she produced a series of drawings of casinos in Las Vegas. Drawing was her only means of recording her experience as it was not permitted to take photographs inside the casinos. The drawings succeeded in capturing the noisy and claustrophobic impression of that environment. In the painting entitled *Slots* with its dark and smoky atmosphere it is impossible to ascertain whether it is night or day; the impression it gives is of 'another world' where time is lost.

These casino drawings marked another stage in her development as she began to experiment with the use of acrylics and pastels. She used pastels to create the drawing of the figure in *Slots*. The pastels were used over a dry acrylic base which proved to be a perfect medium because of its fast-drying qualities thereby maximising speed. Debbie enjoys pastel as it enables an immediate response to what she sees and dispenses with the time needed to mix paint and prepare brushes. It is this element of immediacy that she finds most important in a piece of work, 'I am always more interested in people's sketches rather than their finished paintings because the drawings contain the first spontaneous actions from the impulses of the mind.'

Debbie enjoyed the experience of immersing herself in different cultures. She continued to travel during the late '90s and took her sketchbook to Valencia and Barcelona, where, from her various vantage points, she made a series of very quick, spontaneous sketches of people and their surroundings. Her drawings of passers-by, café and beach life, produced with speed and fluidity of line, effectively captured the moment. Back in the studio, her sketches served to recall the experience she had at the time, so informing the execution of the subsequent painting. In preparation for a painting, Debbie often produces more drawings, overlaying the work with charcoal, pastels and watercolour. Some initial drawing is then made on the canvas with charcoal and pencil and then colour is added. She may emulate the style of the 'action painters' and put the canvas on the floor, pouring or dripping the paint and allowing accidental marks to occur.

In *Barcelona Café*, she succeeds in capturing a vibrant atmosphere of life inside and outside a busy café, whilst from a cloudless sky the Spanish sun burns down. Being quite abstract in her

Zone, 2001, acrylic and pastel on canvas, 152 x 141cms. Collection of the Lowry Hotel

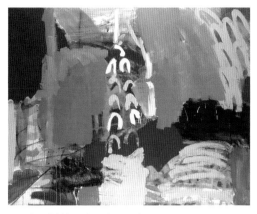

Empire, 2003, oil and pastel
on canvas, 86 x 110cms

I Spy, 2002, oil and pastel on canvas,
168 x 153cms

Collision, 2003, oil and pastel
on canvas, 153 x 153cms

approach, and with an adept use of the materials and brushstrokes, she created a painting that works on many levels to convey the energetic atmosphere of Spanish café life.

Manchester as a subject matter hadn't initially attracted Debbie. Her need to remove herself from the familiar in order to paint and her desire to experience different cultures had taken her travelling, but gradually the excitement of the changing city scene caught her imagination. The regeneration of the city that had begun in the early 1990s fed into the art scene, thereby opening up all sorts of possibilities for local artists and art-lovers.

During her years at MASA studios in the city centre, Debbie focused on her emotional connection with what was around her, and the urban environment became of special interest. Debbie's vision does not lie in recording individual buildings, restaurants and bars; her urban paintings are almost generic. One would not necessarily know, or indeed need to know, which city space was being conveyed. With Debbie's work, the motivation for the piece is always founded on the principles of the abstract expressionist involvement with materials and brushmarks. The city is simply a vehicle through which this is enacted.

Movement is a recurring theme in Debbie's city pieces and one that she can trace back to her early work at college. Perhaps reflecting her own need to be busy and involved, her work usually incorporates the moving figure, very rarely is anyone static. This theme is clearly seen in the drawings she produced in 1999 during a residency at the restaurant, Simply Heathcotes, in the centre of Manchester. The drawings depict the intense activity of the chefs at work. In order to produce these drawings Debbie based herself in the midst of the action in a corner of the kitchen and sketched fervently for over a month, producing a wonderful series of drawings. In the drawing entitled *Chefs,* two figures are bending over a worktop, their forms blend one into the other, both appear to be working together in perfect synchronisation.

In the year 2000, imbued with confidence to push the boundaries and an eagerness to try new materials, Debbie began a series of site-specific painting on glass on the windows at the café, Love Saves The Day, and at Cornerhouse in Manchester. The following year she and several other local artists were invited by Claire Turner and Alison Doocey of Comme Ça PR, an art agency, to produce paintings, sculptures, textiles, photographs, ceramics and jewellery to fill the once defunct Tib Street windows of the Debenhams store. Using special water-based pens, Debbie positioned herself in the window and drew directly onto the glass. She created a drawing entitled *I Spy* in which she captured the events as they happened outside the window during one rainy morning, effectively portraying the hustle and bustle of city life. With the windows lit and a white background to the window space, the light picked up the drawing and projected it onto the back wall. Debbie enjoyed using her drawing technique in a different way. Her work generally consists of different layers of drawing and painting and with this method the glass became another layer.

During this period, Debbie relinquished her teaching posts to concentrate on working at the Tate, Liverpool, as an artistic educator working with a collection of different groups, from young children to inmates of a men's prison. This is an ongoing role which she enjoys as it gives her the opportunity to expand her skills.

Chefs, 1999, screenprint on paper, 14 x 23cms

By the turn of the century Debbie was gaining admiration and popularity as an artist and in 2001 she won a commission to provide a number of huge canvases for The Sorting House in Newton Street, Manchester. The premises, previously the Royal Mail Sorting Office, had been converted into a modern apartment block with a huge central atrium that was a perfect site for her large-scale work. Her brief was to create paintings with a Japanese theme, mirroring the Japanese style

Service Please, 1999, ink on paper, 62 x 81cms

gardens that were being built inside the apartment complex. She took her inspiration from city life in the nearby Northern Quarter and produced four magnificent paintings measuring fourteen feet by three feet. These tall, narrow paintings give reference to the old post office showing snippets of neighbouring buildings and a section of awning from a nearby market stall.

In 2002, Debbie caught the attention of Olga Politzi, an art enthusiast and sister of Sir Rocco Forte, the owner of the five-star Lowry Hotel in Salford. Olga loved the vitality of Debbie's work and commissioned her to produce fifteen huge paintings for her brother's hotel, giving Debbie a free rein to produce the work that was to adorn the dining room, conference room and bedroom corridors. This commission necessitated a move for Debbie from the MASA studios to her own larger premises in Castlefield. Once again she looked to the city for her themes and depicted Manchester life in acrylic and pastel on canvas.

LIVERPOOL JOHN MOORES UNIVERSI
Aldham Roberts L.R.C.
TEL 0151 231 3701/3634

Barcelona Café, 2003, acrylic and pastel on canvas, 105 x 132cms. Private Collection

Barcelona Series 1, 2003, acrylic and pastel on paper, 78 x 97cms

Untitled, 2005, acrylic on canvas, 104 x 109cms

During the same year, a work entitled *Wish You Were Where?*, now on display at Manchester Art Gallery, gave Debbie an opportunity to collaborate with fellow artist Hilary Jack. A commission which Debbie and Hilary applied for and won, *Wish You Were Where?* used the theme of voyages to provide an interactive experience for visitors to the gallery. Debbie and Hilary created a structure made from vintage suitcases, each case representing many stories of travel and adventure. Initially, well-known local figures and artists were sent a luggage label and invited to draw or write about a meaningful and personal travel related story. Amongst those who contributed were Tony Wilson, Johnny Vegas, Badly Drawn Boy, Michael Craig-Martin, Liam Spencer, Martin Murrey, Leo Fitzmaurice, Gina Ward and Sue McCall. Visitors to the gallery then continued the theme, adding their own labels to the mound. Encased in plastic and attached to the cases, the labels have become a whole story in their own right, each one telling a personal and often emotional tale. Originally planned as a two-year installation, the cases are still there four years on and have become so popular that the labels are constantly being replaced by new additions.

Wish You Were Where? seems to be a metaphor which explains the attraction of Debbie's work. Her paintings, like the cases, tell their own intensely personal stories; at the same time, they invite an emotional response in the viewer. A believer in freedom of expression, Debbie's skill is such that her work invites individual interpretation and subjective analysis. The huge positive response confirmed to Debbie the general public's desire for art in their daily, private and working lives.

Further confirmation of the public's desire for art in their working lives came when, in 2005, Debbie received a commission from Stephen Selby of Success Appointments, a recruitment agency, in London to provide art for their new offices. Stephen said 'Having seen Debbie's work in the Lowry in Manchester I was struck by the way she captures vibrancy of life and movement. We are a people-orientated business, and so I felt that her colour and dynamism would portray what we are about. She met the brief for our new offices perfectly, giving us highly visible colour and movement.' What Debbie produced was her signature large-scale canvases in pastel and acrylic, depicting universal city life with the hustle and bustle of figures in the foreground giving the appearance of people pushing up against each other in a race for space. Drawn with very few lines, Debbie's expertise captures the figures' sense of urgency. Her technique offers a sense of distance, the figures appearing both prominent and fleeting within the cityscape.

In the same year Debbie was asked to produce a commission for Peter Holden, an advertising guru for the past forty years, who established his new company, Holden & Friends, in offices in the centre of Knutsford in Cheshire. The commission was for the boardroom and the brief was to bring life and colour to the space. Debbie responded, creating a large-scale, vigorous abstract painting full of vibrant colour and marks. The painting gives reference to urban life with impressions of figures darting back and forth across the canvas through flashes of colour. The painting succeeded in providing an important focal point and popular subject of conversation.

In 2004 Manchester took part in the world's largest public art event, CowParade, which started in Chicago and New York in 1999 and spread to various cities throughout the world. Debbie Goldsmith was the artist first commissioned by Manchester Art Gallery to paint one of these cows in Manchester. The cow, named 'Maverick', was painted with large gestural marks, bursting through one of her abstract paintings on canvas. Other artists then added their cows to the herd and they were placed in various parts of the city. The CowParade in

Manchester ran from June to September and culminated in a grand auction where many of the cows were bought by both public and private collectors with a substantial portion of the proceeds going to charity.

Enjoying the thrill and challenge of placing herself in new situations, Debbie was six months pregnant when, in 2004, she travelled to Brazil after being awarded an Arts Council grant to represent Britain in an exhibition entitled 'Novos Britanicos'. This was the first time an exhibition of European artists in San Paolo had ever been undertaken. It ran for two months and proved to be hugely successful. Debbie went out there for the opening and stayed for two weeks, thoroughly enjoying the experience and appearing in interviews on Brazilian television.

In December of that year, Elijah was born to Debbie and her partner, John Walsh. As with most new parents, their baby provided a new focus in their lives. Debbie remembers those first weeks: 'When Elijah was first born I couldn't think about painting in the way I had done before because I became completely absorbed in the baby.' This feeling lasted for some time whilst Elijah controlled his mother's emotions. Debbie understood and accepted these feelings.

Some artists are able to make artwork based on their experience of birth; I haven't felt the need or desire to do that. I think it is probably because I have always worked in such a way as to be detached from my subject; to be able to look at it objectively in order to recreate it on paper or canvas. However, what becoming a mother did for me was to initiate a re-evaluation of my approach to drawing and painting. The new experience of being a mother feeds into what I do, and although I haven't yet made paintings of Elijah, he influences the way I work in a different way and I couldn't now imagine life without him.

Since the birth of her son, Debbie's focus lies less on the city and more on the prospect of exploring open spaces as her next source of stimulation, highlighting her attraction to a calmer and more reflective phase. Preliminary drawings done in her recent sketchbooks seem to have become more detailed, not so much in an analytical way, but rather in a more observational and emotional way. A possible reason for this, Debbie feels, is that her paintings have become increasingly abstract and complex and this degree of abstraction necessitates more informative preliminary drawings, which she can then unravel. The relationship between these two elements, drawing and painting, has worked so well for Debbie that each will, no doubt, continue to complement the other. The subject matter may change a little but there is no doubt that the energy in her work will remain.

Blue Wall Italy, 2005, oil on canvas, 137 x 76cms

Michelle Leigh

Michelle Leigh is a gentle and quietly spoken person, radiating a calm and centred approach to life, although, in order to pursue her chosen path, she has had to exercise considerable strength and determination. She was born in 1964 in Manchester and brought up within a strict, orthodox Jewish family with a rigid policy of non-integration. When Michelle was about six years old the family left Manchester to join an Israeli kibbutz. She remembers the vastness of the landscape and the red baked earth contrasting with the small figures of her family, as they prepared to return to England after their brief and aborted attempt at making a new life in Israel.

On their return, when Michelle was seven years old, the family moved around the Manchester area in their quest to re-establish themselves in a Jewish community. Michelle's family adhered to firm codes of religious conduct, which meant that she was not able to play with non-Jewish children in the neighbourhood or, indeed, pursue an ordinary childhood outside the home. She felt isolated in the non-Jewish areas where they lived, longing to fit in and be like everyone else. With constantly changing surroundings and the lack of playmates outside school, Michelle became absorbed in reading and drawing. Having lots of siblings prevented her having her own private space within the small family home. With a little corner of the kitchen table as her own territory, she lived in her own private world, spending hours drawing and writing stories as a form of escapism.

With each passing year her parents became more zealous about their religion. In such a strict religious environment, there were firm views about the pre-scribed route Michelle's life would take; as the eldest of six children, it was expected that she would contribute financially to the family and support her brother in his quest for a religious career. As far as her parents were concerned it was barely acceptable for Michelle to pursue her interest in art. Neither university nor a career, least of all in art, would be a viable consideration as there was no precedent for such an eventuality. Instead, the expectation of her entering into an arranged marriage, her life mirroring those of the generations of women before her.

Michelle's dreams, however, did not fit into this tradition. With

Photo by Jennie Keegan

characteristic tenacity, she broke away from the prescribed route and embarked upon an art foundation course at Manchester University. Michelle was fortunate to have the well-respected painter, Don McKinlay (b. 1929) as her inspirational and encouraging tutor. With his assistance Michelle began to explore and develop her painting technique. During this time she focused on portraying the figure and found the ritualistic world of her family's religious home an immensely inspiring, fertile and powerful source of subject matter. She made hundreds of drawings of her four sisters and mother going about their religious life. She used these drawings as a visual diary for the paintings she went on to produce. After successfully completing the Foundation Course, Michelle achieved the Art Foundation Year award for her outstanding work.

The foundation course was followed by a Fine Art degree in Manchester. Whilst still living at home, Michelle continued to be inspired by the subject matter around her. In her own personal studio space at the college she began to use the drawings she had made of her family, pinning them up on the walls around her. *On the Stairwell* painted in 1984, shows a back view of her mother standing on the stairs; she is wearing a headscarf in common with the very orthodox Jewish women who cover their hair for religious reasons. Other family members also feature in the painting; each appears to be in their own private world, with her brother playing the violin. Stairs are present in many of Michelle's paintings, the image being taken from her immediate surroundings and the local synagogue.

A very important painting for Michelle is *Eating Peaches*, 1986. This, for her, denotes a celebration of life and, indeed, of paint. It was inspired by the beginning of spring and paper bags full of peaches. New life and growth is symbolised by the semi-abstract, life-sized figure that is made up of and surrounded by varying tones of peach-coloured paint, thickly applied with hands and brush. She recalls the enjoyment of using the materials to create this painting, and says, 'I experienced a sense of looking beyond my immediate life, unlike the earlier paintings that had a more Jewish theme.' It was a revelation for Michelle to use the single figure as the main focus in the painting. She has, on several occasions, come back to using the single figure in her work and is reminded of the lines from 'Little Gidding' by T.S. Eliot, 'The end of all our exploring will be to arrive back where we started, and to know the place for the first time.'

Matadors, painted in 1986, signifies a tussle, a struggle with life which is symbolised by the almost claustrophobic shrouding of the headscarf on the woman and the trilby worn by the man. Although the figures appear submissive, the overall impact is dominant. Michelle explores her Jewish identity in these works while addressing more universal themes.

Painting, for Michelle, is a language, a vehicle through which she can express her thoughts in a very personal way. During her degree course she often used watercolours as the first reference for oil paintings. She found the process of using them a much more intimate and immediate way to start a piece of work. The function of watercolours, both as works of art in their own right as well as preliminaries for oil paintings, is particularly significant for Michelle. She experimented with a variety of media during her degree course and produced a great deal of work on greaseproof paper, which was inexpensive and easily accessible. Extremely focused and single-minded, Michelle gained a first class honours degree in Fine Art and gained a British Academy Award to fund her Masters Degree in Fine Art at Newcastle University.

Morning of the Wedding, 2001, woodcut, 32 x 32cms

This presented Michelle with the opportunity to leave her home life, with its pressures to conform, and move forward in the direction she had always wanted to take. Her decision to move out of the family home and relinquish her role as a dutiful daughter was regarded as a selfish and shameful act; it created a family rift and was a huge emotional upheaval for Michelle. During the first few months in her new world she experienced a strong sense of dislocation and displacement. She continued to use the rituals from her family life in her work; the symbolic triangular shape of her mother's headscarf appeared in much of her work during this period, as did the back view of her mother with hands raised to welcome the Sabbath and light the traditional candles.

As painting has been a constant focus since her childhood days, providing a secure and constant theme in her life at times of great upheaval, one might think that her paintings have sprung from the oppression she experienced and from her rigid religious background. However, Michele believes that her art is firmly grounded in her zest for painting and joy of using colour. Her focus on her depiction of the rituals in the family home is understandable; it was not so much a statement about the nature of oppression or religious practice, but more the act of recording what she saw around her in her very limited and enclosed world.

Gradually, during her time at Newcastle University Michelle was able to focus on her new

On the Stairwell, 1984,
oil on canvas, 76 x 92cms

Under the Marriage Canopy,
1999, oil on canvas,
58.5 x 79cms

Evening Storm Over Ponte de Lima, Oporto, 1991, oil on canvas, 107 x 153cms

environment. She later learned Buddhist meditation techniques that supported her through a difficult transitional period and helped her to move forward with brighter vision. Instead of paintings centred around her family members she concentrated on producing images of events and people in the local landscape. Still-life paintings and self-portraits also began to emerge.

Towards the end of her master's degree in 1988, Michelle had her first solo exhibition in Cumbria. Included were a number of her very large figurative pieces; dark, sombre paintings with thickly applied oils depicting the world she had left behind. Thinner oils were applied on other paintings giving a less intense feel and a number of watercolours were also included. The exhibition received critical acclaim.

Some of Michelle's inspiration has come from Gwen John (1876-1939), particularly her small, intimate

Eating Peaches, 1986, oil on canvas, 137 x 76cms

paintings, produced with a limited palette. Another source of inspiration is Jan Vermeer (1632–1675) because of his ability to transcend the ordinary, and see beauty in the small details of life. Michelle is interested in those calm fleeting moments that interrupt our busy lives. She also admires Scottish artists and their celebration of colour, which has, to some extent, influenced the more joyous mood within her work.

In 1989 Michelle established herself in a studio on Rochdale Road, Manchester, and with part-time jobs for financial support, she concentrated on developing her work. With a very kind and supportive landlord, Mr Shackleton, who took a painting instead of the rent, Michelle spent three very productive years there. Her work was undergoing a transformation and this was to become the most non-representational period she has ever had. She found that she was unable to use the figure in the same way that she had done previously; her figures had been like characters in a story that she knew very well, but now they needed to be re-defined. *Summer in the City* painted thinly in oil, is much more abstracted. In it, we see suggestions of buildings forming a backdrop against which the fan-shaped headscarf becomes the means by which Michelle explains the figure. Concentrating on colour and shapes, Michelle tried to hint at the suggestion of the human figure without its anatomical form.

In 1992, Michelle left her studio on Rochdale Road and joined MASA (Manchester Artists Studios Association) in Hanover Mill. In the same year she had a very successful solo exhibition at Castlefield Art Gallery in Manchester. Manchester City Art Gallery bought a watercolour for their Rutherston Loan Collection. The exhibition gave her the opportunity to show off the transformation of her work. In the painting she created in 1992 entitled *Her Hidden*, she again portrays her mother in an abstract way, pared down to the minimalist and symbolic headscarf shape. A particularly important painting in this exhibition was *Evening Storm Over Ponte de Lima, Oporto* painted in 1991. Working from sketchbooks and watercolours and painted quite thinly in oil on canvas, this huge piece captures the atmosphere and typical Mediterranean light that often foretells an approaching storm. This painting proved hugely significant for Michelle, in that she had brought figuration back into her work. It portrays the figure of a woman with a pot on her head carrying some produce to market, and the shape of a house in the distance. She no longer felt the need to apply thick paint with her fingers, which had previously resulted in total involvement with her characters, but in this painting she became more of an impartial observer, standing back as would an onlooker of the scene. Revisiting the process of painting figures, Michelle went on to explore it in new ways.

Although Michelle's work was beginning to sell, she had to supplement her income in order to continue the development of her painting. She achieved this by working as a part-time lecturer for the B.A. (Hons) degree in Fine Art at Manchester, Staffordshire and New-castle Universities. While at Hanover Mill, she commuted to London to lead the Art Foundation Experience Course. Michelle recalls, 'We had many interesting characters, includ-ing a London cabbie who was so inspired that he planned to take up his paints and brushes when he relinquished his black cab.' She also worked as a Gallery Educator in the Greater Manchester galleries. Since that time, she has always been involved with art education in one form or another.

Women on the Beach Talking painted in 1997, shows the progression of Michelle's work and the development of the figure. The painting captures a bright, sunny day with two women dressed in bright summer clothes, chatting happily on the beach; it contains none of the angst of some of her earlier work.

In 2000, Michelle's work was exhibited at the Whitworth Art Gallery in an exhibition called 'Times of our Lives', organised as part of the Millennium celebrations. *Beneath the Marriage Canopy* was displayed in 'Rites of Passage', one of the three shows that made up this event. Revisiting the subject matter of her family, the painting centred around the marriage ceremony of one of her sisters, showing the bride and groom under the 'chuppah', the ornate canopy under which Jewish couples are married.

Michelle is also skilled in the technique of woodcuts – one of the first processes she learned as a student. She produces work that is strong and sculptural. The stark contrast of black and white adds to the visual strength of her work. The lack of rich colour and intrica-cies catapults the bold images to the foreground, holding the viewer's gaze like a magnet. Renewing her association with printmaking, she has more recently revisited the etching process.

With a desire to travel, Michelle embarked on a number of trips that were to prove inspi-rational, the most significant being to Prague. Having ancestors from Eastern Europe, she felt a particular yearning to visit the region and once there, was overwhelmed by the beauty and variety of architecture in the old city. Rejoicing in the monumental and grand buildings, she was able to capture their power as a backdrop to the everyday life unfolding before them. Her sketchbook was her constant companion in Prague and, working from her sketches and watercolours, she produced a series of paintings that captured the atmosphere and character of the place with which she feels a particular rapport. It resulted in a successful solo show in 2001 at Salford Museum and Art Gallery which was well received by the press.

In 2003, Michelle's travels to Barcelona and the surrounding countryside culminated in an exhibition at the Wendy J Levy Gallery. Showing small scale, intense, intimate pieces

The Towers of the Old Town Prague, 2001, watercolour, 11.5 x 15cms. Private Collection

Jewish Quarter, Venice, 2005, oil on canvas, 51 x 61cms

Birdcages, Barcelona, 2003, watercolour, 35.5 x 66cms

Outdoor Gossip, Barcelona, 2002, oil on canvas, 82 x 137cms. Private Collection

Outdoor Gossip, Barcelona, 2003, etching and drypoint,
13 x 15cms

The Old Town Square, Prague, 2001, oil on canvas,
76 x 91cms. Private collection

Her Hidden, 1990, acrylic and
watercolour, 107 x 76cms.
Private Collection

together with large, dramatic paintings the exhibition was a visual travel book, taking the visitor on a journey through the landscape. *Outdoor Gossip, Barcelona* shows three chattering girls in the old quarter. The intense light hits the stucco walls of the buildings in the distance and in the foreground, the girls' comfortable relationship provides the human interest that is usually to be found in Michelle's work.

In *Blue Wall Italy* painted in 2005, the figure has undergone another transformation. Painted both dramatically and simply in the foreground, almost larger than life, a young girl seems to occupy the whole of the canvas. However, on the second glance it becomes evident that she is watching two older women who are looking at a newspaper whilst leaning against the distant blue wall of the church. With a wonderful interplay between the vertical and horizontal brushstrokes, the viewer is drawn into the painting.

In *Jewish Quarter, Venice* depicting two religious scholars playing football, Michelle revisits her former religious life with affection and humour. There is a comical element to the work that is kind, not cruel. Although Michelle has let go of this world, it is still very much a part of who she is, having formed her character and her experiences.

She staged a solo show at Stockport Art Gallery in 2005 which included work that spanned a twenty-year period and incorporated the various processes with which she has become so accomplished. Significantly, the exhibition marked the stages in Michelle's own personal journey and development.

Now, with her work in many corporate and private collections across the world, Michelle's work is increasingly popular. Her life as an artist was built on choices that created difficult and emotional experiences. Enhanced by these, her work has moved forward in its vision and accomplishment and receives the recognition it deserves.

Shifting Allegories, 2005, acrylic on canvas, 60 x 60cms

Lisa De Prudhoe

'Every experience in life leaves its own fingerprint.' So believes Lisa De Prudhoe, an outstanding Anglo-American-Panamanian contemporary abstract artist who has certainly accumulated a fascinating array of diverse experiences and adventures. Born in 1963 in Santa Monica, California, to a Panamanian mother and American father, Lisa lived in the U.S. until the age of six when her parents divorced and her mother and British stepfather brought her and brother, Jon, to England. Being uprooted at such a young age and transplanted into a totally different culture and climate had a profound effect on Lisa who struggled with her own identity as a child, not knowing where she belonged and feeling emotionally and physically unsettled. From an early age Lisa attended boarding school in Surrey where she developed a strong feeling of independence but the experience also exacerbated her feelings of difference, dislodgement and displacement.

Whilst growing up in England, Lisa was exposed to the world of art as her mother, the cultural attaché for the Panamanian Embassy, and stepfather owned an art gallery in London. It was there that she met Paolo Serra (b. 1946), an important Italian painter who had a studio in Northampton, where Lisa used to go as a young child. In Paolo's studio, she remembers thinking that one day she wanted to make beautiful paintings just like him and, as an abstract painter, he was hugely instrumental in Lisa's newly found vocation.

In later years, Lisa's mother and stepfather became art publishers and through this, she was introduced to the works of Pablo Picasso (1881–1973), Henri Matisse (1869-1954), Roy Lichtenstein (1923-1997) and Andy Warhol (1928–1987). One of the artists she is most passionate about is Mark Rothko (1903–1970). She admires his use of colour and the way in which the thinly applied paint takes on a luminous quality. She developed a passion for figurative expressionist painters such as Francis Bacon (1909–1992), Lucian Freud (b. 1922) and Willem De Kooning (1904–1997). Lisa vividly remembers going into the house of a friend of her mother in Eaton Square and seeing a huge Francis Bacon triptych. Moved to tears, Lisa knew then for certain that she wanted to become a painter.

With a very influential maternal grandmother who

Photo by Céline Lancien

believed in the value of education, Lisa and her brothers were strongly encouraged to follow a career in law or medicine. Despite her family's involvement in the art world, there was a perverse disapproval of Lisa's desire to study art at university, which was considered a soft option. Not quite knowing what else to do, Lisa began exploring the world with a natural openness to new experiences, welcoming personal freedom and creativity. At the age of twenty she was reunited with her natural father, a former captain in the U.S. Marine Corps and Vietnam veteran. They toured the British Isles, visiting historic literary homes and sharing a common fascination for the work and lives of the Bloomsbury Group.

On returning to London, Lisa studied English and History at University, becoming particularly inspired by the poetry of Emily Dickinson (1830–1886), who, as a repressed New England woman, used to sew her poems into little packages to hide them from her family. During that period, Lisa continued to travel whenever she could and undertook photography as a way to appease her creative thirst. A friend saw the impressive pictures she had taken in Nepal and encouraged her to sell them to a photographic agency which, to Lisa's amazement, paid her £300.

In the summer of 1987 Lisa travelled to Nicaragua to photograph the author, Alice Walker, who was speaking at an international book convention, and got caught up in the mixed ideologies of the ongoing Sandinista revolution, meeting key figures Daniel and Humberto Ortega, and future President, Violetta Chamorro.

After finishing university, Lisa went to India working as a freelance photographer for the British press. This was followed by trips to Egypt and Tanzania where she worked with a scientific expedition for six months. While in Zanzibar, during Ramadan, Lisa was offered a position with the United Nations Development Programme and spent a further two and a half years in Africa. During these years of travel, Lisa immersed herself in each culture. Fascinated by world theologies and Gandhi's quotation, when he said 'God knows no religion', Lisa began to explore the human spirit within Buddhism, Hinduism, Islam, Judaism and the Bantu.

With the completion of her work in Africa, Lisa decided to visit her grandmother in Panama and spend time re-discovering her Latin American roots. It was an exciting time to be in Panama; twenty-one years of military dictatorship had ended and there was the promise of a new democracy. Lisa stayed there for ten months, waiting for reassignment to Africa, during which time she continued working as a photographer for various agencies including Amnesty International, travelling extensively through Central and South America.

The approach of her thirtieth birthday was something of a wake-up call. Despite being a successful freelance photographer, Lisa felt that a critical element was missing from her life. She never lost the desire to become an artist and promised herself that this was what she was going to do. She decided to stay in Panama and started painting; at first depicting images from her Catholic childhood, torturous and angry pictures which gave an insight into her struggles to find herself.

Her first paintings were monochromatic, inspired by the black-and-white tones of photography. Lisa then began recalling the colours from her travels – the tribal cloths and weaves from the Kente kingships. A fellow artist, Roosevelt Diaz (b. 1963), advised Lisa to choose the colour she was most uncomfortable with, use it until she made it her own and fell in love with it. Initially she picked orange – a colour she would have been least likely to use and one that now has become a key element in her palette. Other painters who inspired her use of colour are Alfredo Sinclair (b. 1914) and Olga Sinclair (b. 1957). Lisa recalls, 'they patiently taught me that there was no such thing as an ugly colour, that I only had to look to nature to see that everything combines.'

Lisa's first exhibition was run by the Panamanian Art Council and staged in the dungeons of the old walled city in Panama. Through this exhibition she eventually met Adriano Herrerabarria (b. 1928), a well-respected painter, writer, political commentator and founder of the country's major art schools. Formidable and irascible by reputation, unbeknown to Lisa he visited her exhibition about which he wrote: 'I am not accustomed, for reasons that I won't go into now, to attend art exhibitions. Less so without an invitation! But I deeply pity myself for missing the opportunity of meeting a painter like Lisa De Prudhoe, more specifically her canvases. I can only regret my own extraordinary lack of sensibility and sensitivity in ever hoping to attain De Prudhoe's insight.' Lisa was overwhelmed to have been noticed by this influential man who has visited each of her subsequent exhibitions in Panama and has continued to closely follow her career.

Although none of her work sold for two years, Lisa's determination pushed her to experiment with different subjects and styles whilst making a living by photographing the works of other artists for catalogues. A meeting with Guillermo Trujillo (b. 1927), another Panamanian 'maestro' proved to be another turning point; he persuaded her to embrace abstraction over figuratism.

Lisa's intricate and elaborate backgrounds, painted with minute detail, had always been part of her work. She was asked to paint these as a preliminary surface for another artist, but on seeing the beauty of what she had produced, the artist felt unable to add his own marks to the work, as Lisa's backgrounds had become paintings in their own right. The canvas that

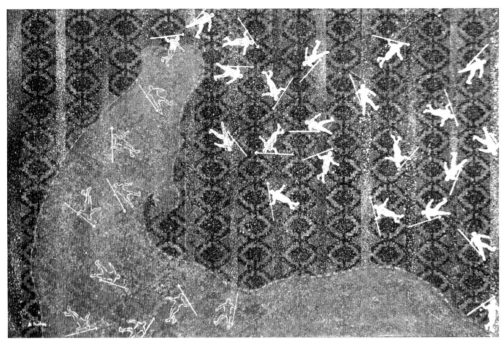

Trojan Horse, 1997, acrylic on canvas, 97 x 148cms.
Collection of James Roark

Exodus I, 1997, acrylic on canvas, 122 x 92cms.
Collection of Justin Humphries

Fragment I, 1997, acrylic on canvas, 148 x 148cms.
Private Collection

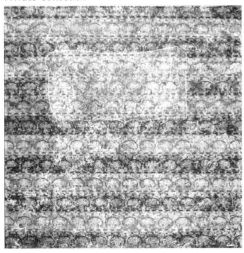

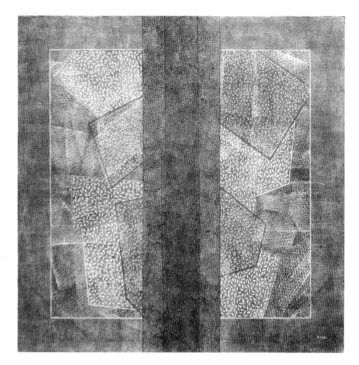

Lares Familiares, 1998,
acrylic on canvas, 200 x 200cms.
Collection of Jorge Sinclair

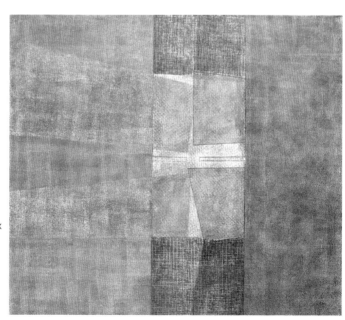

Entretanto, 1998,
acrylic on canvas, 183 x 214cms.
Collection of Mr and Mrs Risseeux

she had produced was two metres square and had taken three months of intensive and concentrated work. The artist suggested that she add her own composition to the background she had created. This led to Lisa designing her 'Falling Men' series. Originally conceived as 'floating' rather than 'falling' figures, they gave movement and depth to the canvas and thus began Lisa's ongoing quest to animate the foreground, which was to lead to her three-dimensional compositions.

In 1997, Lisa's exhibition named 'Fragments' showed the advances made in her work, especially in the relationship between the background and the foreground. Her painting entitled *Trojan Horse* shows the small figures depicting Odysseus's men with their spears whereas *Fragment 1* with its meticulously constructed and detailed background looks like a piece of printed fabric across which subtle bands of colour have been painted. On closer inspection, from the bands of colour emerge dozens of tiny figures, and a blue square painted just above the centre of the canvas has the depth and colour variations of a swimming pool. This exhibition sold out. Not wanting to fall into the trap of producing paintings by formula, Lisa made the final painting in the series, entitled *Exodus*, the only painting in which the 'falling' men are seen upright.

She then started making her paintings much bigger; her work took on a new dimension. During the second half of the 1990s, her artistic profile gradually increased and her work became highly acclaimed with exhibitions selling out before the work had even been displayed.

Detail-conscious, meticulous and perfectionist, Lisa's art provides her with a constant challenge and pushes her forward in a desire to grow. She aligns herself loosely with the Constructivist movement. Originally emanating from Russia in 1913, this school of abstract art is minimal, geometric, spatial and architectural. It uses forms that have a universal meaning rather than subjective, emotional or individual compositions. Constructivism is an art of order, where shapes are pared down to the minimum to express the artist's ideas. Constructivist artists such as Kasimir Malevich (1878–1935) and Aleksandr Rodchenko (1891–1956) were particularly influential in Lisa's paintings where she aspires to pick up the thread of the conversation that they began.

However, there lurks beneath the surface of Lisa's paintings a purity and spirituality that has both cool intellect and warm emotion, adding qualities that reach beyond the somewhat clinical approach of constructivism. Indeed, dichotomy lies at the heart of Lisa's work for there is movement and stillness, peace and turmoil, order and chaos. These opposing forces may mirror Lisa's two universes, the warmth and passion of her Panamanian roots and her more private, restrained British identity.

Lisa's unique canvases are beguiling; the resulting simplicity of the shapes belies the complexity of the process. Lisa loves to produce series of paintings together, all of which will have a theme running through and a coherence and consistency which ensures that the whole is greater than the sum of the parts. Once Lisa has an idea for a series, she will stretch up to twenty-five canvases, preparing them first of all with three or four coats of a waterproof grounding before adding two or three coats of white emulsion. The process ensures that, even by this stage, the canvas has begun to take on a character and tone that are unique to each work. Then, working from detailed drawings she begins to apply the paint to each canvas, a meticulous, time-consuming process taking three or four months to complete each canvas. The paintings are thought-out and planned but still have a life of their own in that they evolve, change colour and shape, so can end up quite different from the way they were intended to be. Using fast drying acrylic paints mixed on a huge three-foot square palette, the paintings are gradually built up by applying ten or twelve layers of intricately painted background, each layer consisting of thousands of tiny brushstrokes, before starting on the foreground. The final painting often consists of forty layers. The resulting geometric juxtapositions are formed from rich layers of colour, with detailed effects such as cross-hatching, which simultaneously veils and distributes the light. There are areas of intense density, but also in places a translucency that is not usually associated with acrylics. Lisa's impressive depth of knowledge as a photographer has informed her use of composition.

Lisa paints her canvases flat on the floor so that she can walk around them and scrutinize them from every angle. Each painting in a series has a 'friend', another painting with which it is paired, creating a further depth of cohesion that will weave through the series.

Lisa experienced a meteoric rise in popularity and success during her time in Panama, with each year heralding a new exhibition. In 1998, an exhibition entitled 'Spaces' saw an absence of the little men figures, replaced by wonderful brushstrokes and textures, so that the shapes seemed to flow into one another. Lisa experimented on some of the paintings in this exhibition by outlining the geometric shapes, although in the painting entitled *Entretanto* its borders remain subtle. In this painting, Lisa perfected her translucent technique and achieved a beautiful glow in the work, so that the painting looks as if it has been executed in oils. *Totem*, another painting included in that exhibition, is devoid of geometric shapes. A review by Pedro Luis Prados, Professor of Philosophy and Ethics at the University of Panama, describes this series: 'the artist develops a series of techniques, eclectic at times, that create an unusual visual universe which seems suspended in the Infinite and which is also loaded with subtle yet dispersed hues.'

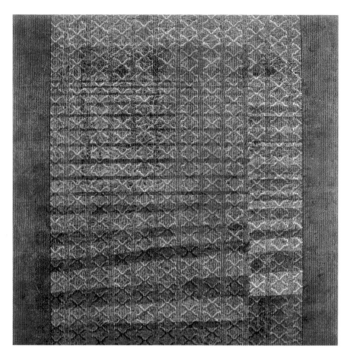

Stairway, 1999,
acrylic on canvas, 200 x
200cms. Collection of Museum
of Contemporary Art, Panama

Totem, 1998, acrylic on canvas, 153 x 122cms.
Collection of Céline Lancien

The Sun also Rises, 1999, acrylic on canvas, 199 x 214cms.
Collection of IBM Central America

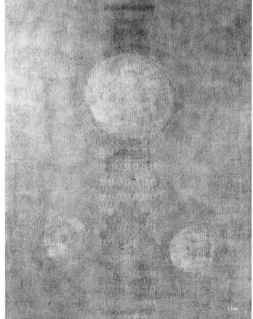

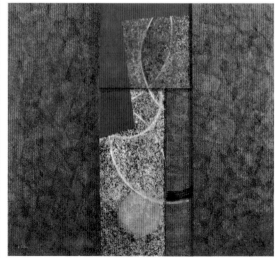

Composición XII, 2001, acrylic on canvas, 153 x 122cms. Collection of Tony Fergo

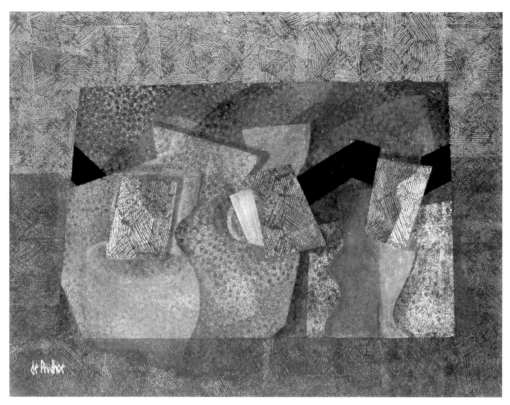

Bodegón, 2000, acrylic on canvas, 92 x 122cms. Private Collection

In 1999, Lisa had an exhibition entitled 'Invocation' at the Museum of Contemporary Arts in Panama. In this series of paintings, one finds echoes of doorways and entrances where the outlines are not drawn but are subtly suggested. The resulting shapes invite the viewer to enter Lisa's universe and discover the hidden depths within. IBM purchased one of the paintings, *The Sun Also Rises*, for their Central American headquarters. *Stairway*, a constructivist painting within this exhibition, became part of the Museum's permanent collection.

In 2000, Lisa had another exhibition in Panama, entitled 'Still Lives'. In these paintings one sees something of a departure from the strong geometric shapes and a move towards a much gentler composition and palette. Wanting to experiment with unfamiliar colours, Lisa used subtle lilacs and greens to suggest elements of vases, cups, glasses and bottles. These are impressive works with the vessels gently floating around the canvas, creating space, form and movement. They have a Cubist quality, and show Lisa's versatility and intuitive grasp of the relationship of one element to another, to the space around and between them and to the canvas as a whole. The work was selling as the exhibition was being hung. A collector liked the work so much that he bought a huge painting and had a special wall built on which to hang it. The exhibition sold out before the show officially opened.

The next day, following a gallery offer, Lisa moved to Melbourne, Australia, amid much critical acclaim for her exhibition in Panama. She exhibited her work for two years in Melbourne whilst simultaneously showing in the U.S. Her interest in the Aboriginal culture influenced her work and her use of colour, more red, reflecting the desert and outback.

'Imaginary Paths', Lisa's 2004 exhibition in Panama, was the culmination of work she produced as a result of her time in Australia and England, and traced her own physical, emotional and spiritual journey. People queued to get into the exhibition and Lisa had to elbow her way through the crowd to get into the gallery. Again, the exhibition sold out immediately, leaving a waiting list of people wanting to buy her work.

Lisa moved to England at the end of 2001 and started working diligently, producing canvases for galleries in Panama, U.K. and U.S. Her exhibition entitled 'Shifting Allegories', shown at the Wendy Levy Gallery in 2006, provided a conceptual link between 'Imaginary Paths', her 2004 exhibition and her next exhibition, 'The Other Side of Silence' in Washington DC in 2007. In 'Shifting Allegories', Lisa used hints of pared down landscapes creating a more minimal and architectural feel to the work. In the title painting, Lisa has arranged the colours in such a way as to convince the viewer that the painting is three-dimensional.

Lisa does not want to determine the viewers' interpretation of her work, preferring that people arrive at their own subjective understanding. Nor does she ultimately want her paintings to have only a visual impact, but rather she hopes that the work will penetrate the subconscious and have a spiritual force, emotionally moving the viewer. Abstract art is complex; it embodies emotion and intellect and can sometimes look simple, but this perceived simplicity belies the huge amount of creation needed in its execution. The work of the Canadian painter, Agnes Martin (1912–2004), has been a constant source of inspiration for Lisa. Martin's early work was geometric, simplified shapes painted in translucent shades and in her later career she sought to create works which could evoke abstract emotions. Her work was influenced greatly by nature, though there was no sense of representation; Martin wanted her viewers to experience the same feelings they have when confronted by nature.

Lisa is fascinated by the concept of synesthesia where one may look at something using one sense, but experience it with another. She is influenced by the modern minimalist composer Philip Glass (b. 1937); Lisa says 'I am interested in polytonality, where music is in more

Dialogo, 1998, acrylic on
canvas, 200 x 200cms.
Collection of Inter-Oceanic
Museum of the Canal,
Panama City

Still Life, 1999, acrylic on
canvas, 199 x 214cms.
Collection of Eloy Alfara

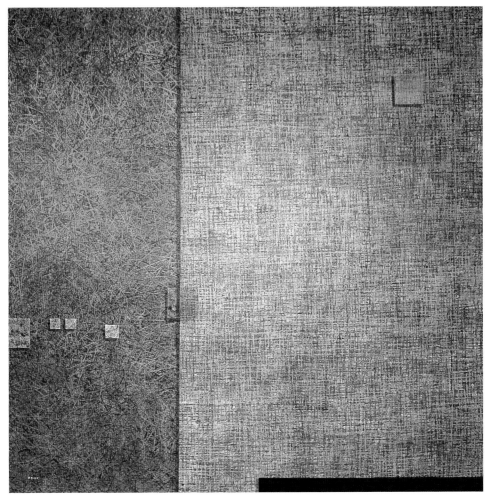

The Other Side of Silence, 2006, acrylic on canvas, 210 x 210cms

than one key simultaneously, and in the ambiguities that this language can create. I am working towards transferring this aural concept into its visual equivalent.' With this in mind, the senses of the art world will be further stimulated by the future work of Lisa De Prudhoe.

Party Party, 1987, etching and aquatint, 46 x 49cms

Julia Midgley

Julia Midgley's professional career is full and colourful. Since early art-school years her commitment to drawing and painting as a means of communication has remained a constant focus. She is recognised as an established documentary and fine artist who has succeeded in building a reputation as a respected professional. Amongst other achievements she is a fellow of the Royal Society of Painter Printmakers (R.E.)

Julia was born in 1948 in Manchester. The family lived in Knutsford, Cheshire, where she spent her childhood. Having a natural talent for observing and drawing what was happening around her, she predictably focussed on studying art. In 1964 she embarked on a two-year pre-diploma course in Northwich, Cheshire before going to what was then the Manchester College of Art and Design, in 1966. As drawing was her natural strength she decided to specialise in illustration, gaining a Dip.A.D. in 1969.

In the same year Julia moved to London, working as a freelance illustrator on a number of projects ranging from book covers to advertisements. However, the need to conceptualise and the constraints of working to someone else's brief meant that there was little room for Julia's own creative vision and she ultimately felt that the role of illustrator was not her natural way forward. Following her father's death in 1972, she moved back to Cheshire and in 1973 she married Jonty Godfrey, an architect, whom she had known since student days in Northwich.

From 1976 to 1979 Julia exhibited her work around the north west of England, including the Elf Oil Competition in Manchester and the National Print Exhibition in Blackpool. Her dedication to drawing from both the life model and the human skeleton enabled her to make skilful drawings at the Northern Ballet School in Deansgate, Manchester. The drawings at this time were executed in pencil or pastel on carefully selected paper. Julia continues to be particular regarding the correct choice of paper for her subject matter.

During the 1980s there was a growing demand for her work. Her first solo show at Salford Art Gallery in 1982 included drawings she had made directly from observation at the Royal College of

Photo by David Heke

Leopards in Landscape, 1996, acrylic and pastel, 70 x 125cms. Private Collection

Horse in French Landscape, 1997, acrylic and pastel, 76 x 95cms. Private Collection

Operation, 1999,
acrylic and pastel,
95 x 120cms.
Collection of the Royal
Liverpool & Broadgreen
University
Hospital Trust

Emergency A & E,
1999, 28 x 30cms,
ink and acrylic

LIVERPOOL JOHN MOORES UNIVERSITY
LEARNING SERVICES

Music where musicians were captured in total accord with their instruments. At the Grundy Art Gallery in Blackpool, her second solo exhibition at the Grundy was based on a trip she had made to the United States, where the West Coast colours influenced her work. An increasing interest in Egyptian sculpture led Julia to make drawings in the British Museum, and some of this work was included in an exhibition of her work, in 1982, at the Business Art Galleries in London, a gallery partly owned by the Royal Academy.

Much of Julia's long and successful career has been devoted to working as a documentary artist. This genre has very specific requirements and demands particular skills of draughtsmanship. Her first commission came from Tony Clegg, Chairman and Chief Executive of Syltone Plc, Yorkshire. After visiting Julia's exhibition at the Business Art Galleries he invited her to produce a series of drawings based on his factories in Bradford. Initially, the concept was to make drawings depicting life on the factory floor in preparation for larger works that were to hang in the boardroom and reception. Those initial drawings proved popular in their own right and were purchased along with the completed larger works.

Julia feels that the most straightforward aspect of being a documentary artist is actually producing the drawings. The difficult part is being unobtrusive and taking care to avoid causing any disruption in the workplace. The skill in capturing the essence and atmosphere of the scene is dependent on the artist's ability to carefully edit and manipulate the image in order to keep it interesting. The advantage of a drawing over a photograph is that a drawing can record events that take place over several minutes or hours, whilst photographs can only capture fractions of a second.

Documentary artists provide a social commentary relating to events in front of and behind the scenes in everyday life. They describe a specific experience or set of circumstances in such a way that depth and richness are added to our general understanding and perception of life; a visual archive is created. There are a number of artists in this field who, like Julia, have derived their subject matter from direct observation in unlikely surroundings. One of the most important artists of the first half of the twentieth century was Paul Nash (1889–1946) best known for the images he produced of both the First and Second World Wars as an official war artist whilst continuing to develop and promote his personal style of painting. Another artist who successfully recorded life and events of the twentieth century was Feliks Topolski (1907–1989) who embraced the life around him and portrayed it in such a way as to communicate the essence of what he saw. A quote by Feliks Topolski illustrates his acute awareness of life: 'The airless studios grow stifling. Kick the door open – the hum of life turns into a roar.'

During her career, Julia has been involved in several documentary projects; in 1992 she was invited and taken by the police to record events at Aintree Racecourse on Grand National Day. She was invited back the following year by Peter Greenall (now Lord Daresbury) to record the three-day race meeting; she received a commission for another sporting event when Bernstein PLC commissioned her to produce drawings of the 1994 Wimbledon Lawn Tennis Championships.

The Royal Liverpool and Broadgreen University Hospital Trust presented a challenging commission; her residency at the Liverpool Hospital between 1997 and 1999 was the result of a conversation with Professor Robert Sells, the eminent transplant surgeon. Julia recorded life at the hospital through drawings that captured scenes from the operating theatres, emergency wards, pharmacies and physiotherapy departments. Julia has often been asked if she felt queasy in those intense hospital environments; she explains that the absorbing nature of the events demanded total concentration if the drawings were to succeed. Julia was allowed to use only pencil in the operating theatre; the addition of ink or watercolour took place later in her studio.

The drawing entitled *Tender Farewell* shows the emotional impact of a death on the medical staff. Here, there is no distraction of medical equipment. A single staff member attends a swathed body, pausing to reflect; on her face there is an expression of intense sadness. In *Emergency A & E* there is no time to pause and reflect; here the medical staff are propelled by the urgency of the situation.

In 1967, as a student, Julia had applied to Granada Television to work on the set of 'Coronation Street' in order to produce some behind the scene sketches as part of her course. Little did she know then that thirty-three years later, she would return. From July 2000 until May 2001, as part of the 'Year of the Artist' initiative, Julia was Artist in Residence at Granada Television's Regional Programmes Department in Manchester. This project, sponsored by the North West Arts Board, gave Julia an opportunity to observe and record the frenetic activity of those working in television. The spontaneity and immediacy of Julia's drawings synchronised perfectly with the fast pace and tight deadlines of life in television. Drawing directly onto a variety of handmade tinted papers she used dip pens and acrylic inks to heighten the graphic effect. With access to the newsroom, studios, edit suites and production galleries, as well as numerous locations, Julia captured the personalities of those familiar faces that appear regularly on the television screen together with the technicians working behind the scenes.

Serious and tense moments came at the end of the Granada Television residency when, in June 2001, the results of the general election became clear. William Hague stood down as leader of the Conservative Party. Julia's drawing captures the atmosphere of the journalists in the newsroom conferring with each other as a grim-faced Hague can be seen on the monitor. This final drawing, with hand-written text, was rushed to the printer in Liverpool who was waiting for the final page of the book, *Granada Sketchbook*, which would accompany the residency and touring exhibition.

In 2000 Julia accepted a second 'Year of the Artist' residency alongside the Granada project. This was at Blackpool Pleasure Beach, commissioned by Blackpool Pleasure Beach Ltd and NorthWest Arts Board. Julia made drawings of the various rides and entertainment as well as the responses and expressions of the general public. Many of these images have been recalled in much later work.

Her most recent project was a residency during 2004 at Chester's Roman Amphitheatre. Julia says,

> Archaeologists are hands-on people, interested in artefacts and marks left by previous generations. Their work demands a measured and careful procedure, often in difficult conditions. They must be capable of working long solitary hours as well as frequently belonging to a larger team: parallel to the working conditions of an artist, where many spend their entire working lives looking at and making marks, referring to history, recording their work and using their hands to produce an end product. Whilst artists tend in the main to work alone, they too, by necessity often need to work alongside others, galleries, framers, publishers and so on.

> I have enjoyed many challenging residencies and worked for a wide variety of clients. It is my job to record, with drawings, the everyday working lives of others. I become a fly on the wall who must, without causing any distraction, produce an informed and sympathetic portrayal of the work taking place. It is necessary to develop a sound understanding of subject matter in order to properly portray it. This means that questions must be asked but only when, in this case, the archaeological investigation work would not be disturbed. Thus break times and end-of-day discussions became important opportunities to extract information about the work in progress.

> My working methods are very simple. I try to avoid using a camera, preferring instead to draw directly on to a wide variety of tinted handmade papers. I carry a toolbox containing acrylic inks, dip pens, pencils, and other useful bits and pieces. A folding stool, flask and packed lunch complete the kit. I do carry a small camera with me but tend to use that only for complicated detail which may need to be replicated later.

> Local media and regional television crew were frequent visitors to the archaeological site

David Heke Photographs the Survey, 2004, acrylic and acrylic ink, 28 x 38cms

and the BBC's 'Timewatch' programme was there for the entire summer. A drawing she made, entitled *David Heke Photographs the Survey*, is an example of Julia recording the recorder.

Julia enjoys capturing unusual or bizarre elements. The archaeologists were bemused by her fascination with the battered and rusty *Alan's Skip*, but Julia found the image particularly graphic and strong. She was similarly attracted to the unlikely sight of a row of upturned wheelbarrows, eventually realising that when the workers went for a break, their tools would be stored beneath the upturned barrow. Whilst the team of archaeologists assumed that the focus of interest would be the unearthed objects themselves, Julia's observations show the more 'human' aspects of what was going on.

A fundamental interest in human nature underpins Julia's documentary projects as she seeks to emphasise the reality of people's lives. She has been influenced for many years by the political artist Sue Coe (b. 1951), a graphic witness to the plight of the troubled, overlooked and downtrodden in society. Since 1997, Julia has been a Reader in Documentary Drawing at Liverpool School of Art and Design, part of Liverpool John Moores University, and has had a consistent and continuing career within this genre.

However, there is another aspect of Julia's work that allows her a more creative freedom; her drive is to produce work that breaks new ground using a personal language to reflect her experiences. This can be seen in her series of horse drawings. Julia grew up with horses and has never lost her love for them. As a child she was struck by an image, by Franz Marc (1880 –1916), of a blue horse drinking water from the river. Her drawings of horses have become a creative vehicle through which she can express aspects of her life. She uses subject matter that appeals to her intellectually as well as visually; these elements produce an image which, for her, is personally meaningful.

Arguably one of her most personal pieces is *Celebration*. This symbolic and surreal piece was produced using acrylic and pastels and was begun in 1990 whilst she was pregnant with her younger son, Raphael; a pregnancy that necessitated some time in hospital owing to complications. It took over a year to complete this intriguing piece which depicts elements of her life at that time. Her elder son, Oscar, is portrayed in two forms; in both images he is shown wearing a favourite Panda mask. The pregnant Julia is portrayed floating gracefully in the sky and again in a skating position, a reference to one of her favourite paintings, *The Rev. Robert Walker Skating on Duddingston Loch* by Sir Henry Raeburn (1756–1823). Julia's quirky sense of humour can be seen in her choice of headgear for the skating form; it is the bedpan that became part of her daily life whilst unable to move from her hospital bed. The flying male figure is an amalgamation of references. Whilst representative of her husband, it was also informed by the sculpture situated at Manchester Airport, *The Ascent of Man* by Dame Elizabeth Frink (1930–1993). The bird figure in the painting is another amalgamation of references; based on a sculpture she purchased by Indian artist Dhruva Mistry (b.1957), it is a direct reference to an Egyptian sculpture of a bird in the British Museum. In the foreground of the painting is a magnificent white horse, a reference to the Spanish Riding School in Vienna. Julia called this painting *Celebration* in recognition of the safe delivery of her son, Raphael.

Cavalcade celebrates all the different horses that have brought her lifelong pleasure, from the white Wade china horses she collected as a child, to ancient sculptures of horses in Venice and Rome, and a galloping fairground horse. Her gymkhana days are represented by a cossack in a mounted fancy dress event. Julia prefers to use plinths and a chessboard motif instead of a conventional background.

The drawing, *Escape from the Plinth*, was inspired by ancient Chinese sculptures of horsemen. Rendered immovable and imprisoned by their sculptor, Julia made this drawing of their escape and liberated them.

Friend or Foe depicts an encounter between a horse and a leopard and signifies the shift in Julia's focus from one body of work to another. Having seen ebony and ivory carvings of leopards in the Queen's Collection at the Museum of Mankind, Julia decided to bring images of leopards into her work, again as a way of describing a personal situation. The depiction of the horse lying down reflects Julia's relative confidence with her body of work, when an interloper in the form of the leopard arrives to threaten the status quo. In this composition, Julia's use of the shadows is significant, the horse and leopard look more confrontational in their shadow portrayal than in real life, heralding the apprehension that accompanies change. In *Conversation* the shadows of the leopard and horse are united; hurdles and obstacles relating to change have been overcome.

Conversation, 1994, acrylic and charcoal, 72 x 90cms

Friend or Foe, 1993, acrylic and pastel, 85 x 108cms

Julia is also an accomplished printmaker, favouring the etching technique. *Masque*, an etching with aquatint, is a complex and highly effective composition incorporating a number of personally meaningful themes. The masked figures were influenced by the Venice exhibition at the Royal Academy and the Venice Festival of Masks. This reflects Julia's continuing fascination for masks, wigs and hats. Her elder son, Oscar, is seen on a swing held by two masked angels. The scene is viewed from above; whirling winged horses, their tails flying, lead the onlooker's eyes around the work to generate a sense of movement. In order to draw flying horses seen from above, Julia visited an equine swimming pool, where she was able to look down on the horses as they swam, to provide the relevant reference. Her skill in etching has its foundations very firmly rooted in her draughtsmanship. She has described drawing as the 'bedrock' of her work.

Julia has several times been an exhibitor at the Royal Academy of Arts' Summer Exhibition. On one such occasion, in 1987, she exhibited her etching, *Party, Party* which

Celebration,
1990-91,
acrylic and
pastel,
70 x 125cms

Rides A Go Go,
2001,
mixed media,
75 x 95cms.
Private
Collection

Bingo, 2003, mixed media,
95 x 124cms

Escape from the Plynth,
2004, acrylic and pastel,
94 x 94cms

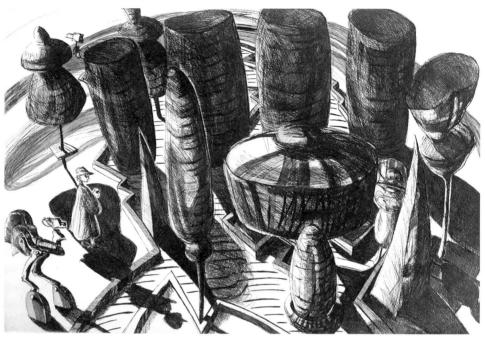

Secret Garden, 1995, etching and aquatint

brings together people from all sorts of different eras and professions to congregate at an unlikely gathering. Old music-hall characters, taken from a book left to her by an elderly aunt, talk to characters from art history. Mingling amongst them are people she has sketched in trains and bars and all are observed by three stone monkeys which are actually Egyptian sculptures in the Louvre.

In 1996 Julia won a prize at the Printmaker's Council National Open Competition for her etching with aquatint, entitled *Secret Garden*. She was awarded a week's residency at Gainsborough's House Print Workshop where she used the sketches she had made a few months earlier, in Provençe, to develop two etchings; the first depicted the strange form of Mont St Victoire, near the home of the painter Paul Cézanne (1839–1906), with Julia's customary horse and leopard in the foreground. The second etching shows the summit of this mountain upon which Julia has placed objects from Cézanne's studio. In the same year she was awarded the Rainford Trust Prize for painting.

The painting entitled *Bingo* depicts the culmination of a period from 2000 to 2002 in Julia's working and personal life. Within the setting of the bingo hall in Huyton, Merseyside, (where she had been Artist in Residence as part of the Liverpool Biennial), she placed images of a kangaroo and a dingo which were inspired by a visit to Australia. The curving rail at the top of the work was taken from Blackpool Pleasure Beach. In the foreground, jugglers' clubs are being thrown into the air by two figures dressed as pink rats. These figures were seen at a Blackpool Pleasure Beach Bonfire Night party. Two arresting sculptures like human beanbags feature in the foreground; these acknowledge the work of the Spanish sculptor, Juan Muñoz (1953–2001).

Masque, 1989, etching and aquatint, 35 x 25cms. Private Collection

Currently Julia's work reflects those tiresome irritations of working life which intrude on productive studio time such as form-filling, conference attendance, reports, grant applications, committee meetings and so forth. Julia hoards many images, dropping them into her memory bank and sketchbooks to be retrieved and used later. Her interest in human nature coupled with her intelligence and sense of humour provide all the material she needs to continue recording her personal view of life.

Julia's artistic skills also won her the 1993 and 2000 Laing Landscape Northern awards. She is a member and past vice-president of the Manchester Academy of Fine Arts (M.A.F.A.), a member of the Printmakers Council, as well as a member of the Cheshire Artists Network (C.A.N.), and the Chelsea Arts Club.

Intra Muros II, collagraph with chine collé, 27 x 27cms

Patricia Niemira

Childhood memories, images and themes have provided Patricia Niemira with a wealth of inspiration for her work. She was born in Nottingham to an Irish mother and a Polish father, both strict catholics. Her father had been a pilot in the Polish airforce and had stayed in England after the war. Patricia's upbringing was filled with religious images that were to have a strong influence on her work. Patricia was only six years old when she suffered the tragedy of her mother's lengthy illness. At this tender age she made drawings to send to her mother to brighten her long days in hospital. Her mother's subsequent death at only thirty years old, left the young Patricia and her even younger sister, Olenka, in the care of a heart-broken father trying to overcome his grief and continue to work hard in order to support his children. Patricia often spent many hours alone, drawing and reading and escaping into her imagination. In the fullness of time, her father remarried and had four more children, creating a large, lively family.

With a strong belief in the power of education, Patricia's father was focused on her academic development and hoped that she would, some day, become a doctor. Patricia was not attracted to the sciences and much preferred the arts and languages. She attended a convent school in Manchester, and it was during a visit to Manchester Art Gallery as part of the 'A' - level syllabus that her desire to pursue art was strengthened. She enjoyed being surrounded by so many wonderful works of art and, in particular, the allegorical Pre-Raphaelite paintings. The works of these and similar artists served to provide a bridge between her religious youth and the development of her understanding and love of art. One of her favourite artists at that time was Holman Hunt whose works, such as *The Scapegoat* and *The Light of the World*, were resonant with religious beliefs and imagery.

With the enthusiastic support and encouragement of her art teachers, it was thought that Patricia would be destined to go to Art College when she left school, but a strict catholic upbringing and lack of confidence at that stage left Patricia feeling ill-equipped to enter the liberal world of an art student. Instead, she found herself taking up clerical employment which was to last for three years.

Photo by Alan Birch

Winter Vista, collagraph, 16 x 11.5cms

However, the desire to develop her artwork remained strong and wanting to work within the art environment led her to embark on a three-year course at Mather Teacher Training College, Manchester, taking art as her main subject. After qualifying in 1972 she began to teach classes of infants before pursuing further studies and subsequent qualifications, gaining an M.A. in 1989 in teaching art within the special education sector. She then began a long and extremely fulfilling career teaching art to children with learning difficulties. In this role, Patricia's natural enthusiasm and love of art enabled her to provide her pupils with an outlet through which they could express themselves, using a whole variety of media and materials.

Patricia taught for a further 27 years whilst continuing to develop her art and maintained her desire to become a full-time artist. She gleaned a great deal of pleasure from enabling others to express themselves through art but eventually decided to give more consideration to her own artistic development and began taking lessons from William Turner, a respected artist who worked from his studio in Cheadle Hulme. He taught her to paint in oils by copying paintings that had been produced by old masters. As her confidence grew, Patricia joined Stockport Art Guild in 1989, a move which was to become a turning point in her career as an artist. Here, she began life drawing classes and started to enter open competitions. She enjoyed being with others who shared a mutual enthusiasm for art and took inspiration from the work of more experienced artists. Patricia then joined the Open College of the Arts where her skills were further developed. It was in 1993 when she attended a drypoint workshop led by Alan Birch at the Whitworth Art Gallery that her interest in printmaking began.

'Drypoint is an intaglio technique like engraving, in which the image is drawn on a metal plate with a needle, raising a ridge that prints a soft line. Drypoints are usually small editions. This is because the drawing that has been scribed into the plate begins to lose its clarity after it has passed several times through the roller press.' An early drypoint monoprint, Afternoon Light, Manchester Cathedral II, shows the cathedral bathed in soft evening light.

With her increasing interest in printmaking, Patricia decided to explore the technique of etching using the facilities provided by Alan Birch at the MASA studios in Hanover Mill. She enjoyed the unpredictability she encountered when printmaking; 'There are so many variables in the process that the end result can be quite surprising.' Patricia describes the process of making an etching as follows:

The procedure begins by coating a metal plate with a ground, usually wax, that resists acid. A design or image is then drawn into the wax using a sharp tool or needle so that the wax is removed from the plate only where the tool touches the metal. The plate is then submerged in a bath of acid which bites into the exposed metal, so etching the

Afternoon Light, Manchester Cathedral II, drypoint, 30 x 12cms

Near Grindleford, collagraph, 13 x 9cms

A Quiet Lane, collagraph, 10 x 17cms

The Old Tree, collagraph,
17 x 9.5cms

Into the Country II, collagraph, 17 x 11cms

drawing into the plate. The wax or 'ground' is then completely removed to reveal a metal plate with a drawing or image etched into it.

Patricia then used aquatint to give a tonal quality to her work. This process involves recoating the plate with a powdered resin. The plate is heated over a flame which melts the resin to coat the plate. This produces a textured ground which holds the ink. Tones are created by systematically dipping the plate in acid after having 'stopped out' areas with an acid resistant varnish. The plate is then ready to be inked. Once it has been inked the image is transferred onto a piece of damp printmaking paper by means of passing the plate, with paper on top, through a roller press which forces the ink from the etched plate onto the paper. The plate has to be re-inked for each print. Patricia began to use this technique to produce a series of

Through the Glass Darkly, mezzotint, 13 x 17cms

Ah! Now I Know What It Is To Shudder,
etching, 18 x 14cms

images based on children's nursery rhymes and fables. Her ongoing love of these childhood story images can be seen in much of her work; Patricia believes that in some way she is trying to create through these images a vision of the idyllic childhood that she was denied through the loss of her mother.

Patricia's earliest memories are of sitting on her mother's knee reading and looking at pictures in story books; it is understandable that she would want to recreate such moments. With inspiration from Arthur Rackham's many wonderful illustrations of children's stories, Patricia worked on etchings of Grimm's Fairy Tales. Her work conveys a gentle humour and beauty and the non-threatening yet fearful thrill which forms the essence of many children's stories and illustrations. Patricia has also been influenced in this type of work by the prints of Paula Rego whose illustrated nursery rhyme book she particularly admires. Patricia says 'Some of Rego's images have a surreal, sinister and menacing quality, which simultaneously frighten and fascinate.' Initially winning acclaim in Portugal for her semi-abstract paintings that sometimes included collage elements, Rego reinterpreted the folktales of her childhood using an adult language. *Ah!*

Enigma Variation, collagraph, 17 x 32cms

Now I Know What It Is To Shudder, taken from Grimm, is one of Patricia's earliest etchings and perfectly conveys these various influences.

With her growing interest and success in printmaking, Patricia expanded her repertoire of printing techniques by attending Hot Bed Press workshops at the Whitworth Art Gallery. Particularly through the collagraph technique she found a favourable process that enables her to express her personal interpretation of the world.

> Collagraphs can be made in different ways using a variety of materials. My favoured method of working is to use a piece of silver-faced card as a base for a collage plate. The plate is created by scratching directly onto the card with a sharp tool, thereby scoring the card. I then create texture by attaching found materials such as netting, string and torn paper, enhanced by the addition of acrylic textured pastes and glue. I next apply different coloured printing inks to the plate in a painterly manner using scraps of mountboard as paintbrushes. Dampened paper is then placed on top before being passed through the press, the resulting impression being one of embossing as well as printing, combining texturing with the layering of colour.

In this process, Patricia can indulge her love of collecting and recycling found objects to construct a still life or a landscape.

Into the Light, collagraph with chine collé, 27 x 27cms

Landscape III, collagraph, 9 x 13cms

It has never been Patricia's intention to produce a direct representation of the landscape, as she explains

My works reflect a personal interpretation of the world around me. Some subjects allow for lengthy observation, for example, flowers in the garden, household objects or informal still-life studies. Other subjects are caught as fleeting images, observed as I travel from place to place. These subjects are committed to memory, or captured as thumb nail sketches to be brought together to form a representation of the mood or feeling evoked by the initial observation.

The results are little gems; enticing and atmospheric. *Into the Country II* shows the Derbyshire countryside where a twisting path leads the viewer's gaze to the distant hills.

The Old Tree captures the countryside near Sheffield where the typical grey stone walls contrast with the lushness of the fields. This print is a good example of an accidental, but pleasing, result of the collagraph process. Patricia has allowed a little of the glued materials to escape from the perimeter of the plate, adding an extra interest to the picture. A collagraph printed from the same plate can have many variations. This is a feature of the process that Patricia enjoys.

The late Terry Kirman was a strong early influence. Having been very impressed on seeing a demonstration of his colourful work, Patricia spent a week at Whalley Abbey in Blackburn where Terry was artist in residence. He encouraged the development of her work and it was as a result of Terry's vibrant use of colour that Patricia came to dislike using pure black pigment, preferring instead to mix her own black ink for printing.

Through the Glass Darkly is an early mezzotint which shows the result of her desire to mix her own black inks. This can be compared to *Ah! Now I Know What It Is To Shudder* which was printed using a conventional pure black ink. Producing a mezzotint is a very laborious process but the effort is rewarded by the soft graduations of richness of tone and the velvety quality of the inks. Mezzotint is an intaglio process and is a reversal of the normal printmaking technique in so much as the image is worked light out of dark. *Through the Glass Darkly* shows Patricia's interest in imaginative themes. A hybrid animal resembling those to be found in children's fairy tales is seen in front of a framed window through which we view a bleak landscape.

In 2001 Patricia won the Derbyshire Print Trophy at the Derbyshire Open Competition at Buxton Museum and Art Gallery for the second time. The winning print, *Landscape III*, is a collagraph depicting a picturesque scene in Derbyshire. In the same year Patricia first encountered the South of France when she drove there to visit two of her sisters, passing through the picturesque town of Beziers with the river running through its centre and its medieval castle and surrounding vineyards, Patricia had felt that it would be a wonderful place to have a studio. A twist of fate intervened when, a month after returning home from her visit, she discovered that Stockport Art Gallery was looking for a local artist to represent the town at an exhibition called 'Visual Arts of Here and Elsewhere' in its twin town of Beziers. Patricia applied and was accepted. She exhibited her work at Beziers' Museum of Fables and Stories along with artists from Beziers' other twin towns of Russia, Spain, and Germany; artists from France and Holland were also invited to exhibit.

Patricia was so attracted to the area that the following year she remortgaged her home in England to buy a village house in the Haut Languedoc Regional National Park not far from Beziers. In 2003, she realised her ambition and gave up teaching to become a full-time artist, setting up her main studio in France where she lives and paints during the summer months. When in England Patricia uses the printmaking facilities at Hot Bed Press and at Alan Birch's studio in Waterfoot, Rossendale.

In 2004, her collagraph *Enigma Variation* was exhibited at the Manchester Academy Open Exhibition at Salford Art Gallery and was joint winner of the John White Small Print Award.

Her latest development within printmaking has been the technique of chine collé, a method of combining coloured papers and printmaking. Her most recent prints are collagraphs with chine collé, examples of which are *Into the Light* and *Intra Muros II*.

Patricia has also recently embarked upon a very different project. Wanting to learn more about her Polish father's background, she visited Poland in 2005 to meet up with relatives and visit the farm in Zareby Koscielne, in the north-east of Poland, where her father was brought up. She has also contacted her late mother's elderly sister and is embarking on a journey with both sides of the family that will fill in many of the gaps in her knowledge and memories of her childhood. To tie in with this project, she has begun a series of drypoints using reference material obtained from Irish and Polish relatives.

An elected member of Manchester Academy of Fine Art and a Member of the Hot Bed Press, Patricia is continuing to develop her work as she enjoys inspiration from the landscapes of both England and France, although there remains the fear that, due to Patricia's love of the Mediterranean lifestyle, we may one day lose her to the South of France.

Castlefields, etching and aquatint, 24 x 24cms

Frances Seba Smith

Frances Seba Smith's diverse art reflects her energy, curiosity and constant exploration of the world. As with many artists Frances is skilled in the use of a variety of media, but she fundamentally sees herself as a printmaker. She was born Frances Seba McGuinness in 1935 in Montreal, Canada, where she lived until the age of twenty four.

She began to draw at a very young age, sketching groups of people at childhood birthday parties and drawing her brother while he played ice hockey. Her talent must have been evident in those early years as her primary-school teacher kept a collection of her sketches. When she was about ten years old, Frances attended Saturday morning art classes at the Montreal Museum of Fine Arts, run by Arthur Lismer who was one of the famous 'Group of Seven'. These were the first artists to actually go out and portray the Canadian Wilderness. At the end of each class she would sneak into the museum to look at the paintings by El Greco whose work mesmerised her.

After finishing high school Frances went to art college and took a graphic design course in publicity at the École des Beaux Arts in Montreal, where she was introduced to printmaking. In her final year she won a national design competition, open to all art colleges nationwide, organised by the Advertising Council of Canada. Following her graduation Frances went to work for a small design studio but was soon head-hunted by Sun Life Assurance Company of Canada. She designed all the company's promotional material, for which she went on to win three advertising awards.

In 1956 Frances met her future husband, Tony Smith, through a common interest in sailing. They married in Canada one year later and in 1959 came to England and settled in Walton, Cheshire where their three children were born, moving six years later to Cuddington, Cheshire. While her children were young, Frances worked from home on portrait commissions, mainly in pastel, then later embarked on a degree in Fine Arts at North Staffordshire Polytechnic. After exploring all types of artistic media she decided to specialise in printmaking. As a mature student Frances thoroughly enjoyed her three years in Stoke-on-Trent, graduating with a first-class honours degree in

Iron Bridge, etching, 24 x 24cms

Bridgewater Canal, etching, 22 x 25cms

1982. Following her degree she taught art at Stoke-on-Trent Sixth Form College. Teaching came naturally to her, enjoying the interaction with the pupils and fostering their imagination with all kinds of exciting projects. She then went on to teach printmaking at Crewe and Alsager College (now part of Manchester Metropolitan University).

In 1990 Frances had a studio built, equipped with an antique Albion press and an etching press. She ran weekend art courses which proved to be extremely popular. However, the success of these courses led to a huge infringement on her time. She decided to end the weekend courses and concentrate solely on her own work.

Tarxien Lady,
oil on canvas
49 x 51cms.
Private Collection

Ancient Artifacts,
etching and monoprint,
53 x 45cms

Victorian Manchester, etching, 24 x 31cms

Water Womble, etching, 25 x 30cms

Canal Basin, etching, 22 x 25cms

From 1983 she became an ardent exhibitor of her work, showing in many solo and group exhibitions in the north-west as well as in London, Wales, Canada and Malta, later showing in Russia, France and Italy. Her work has been exhibited many times in Malta, in private galleries and in the Museum of Fine Arts. She is enthused by the history, architecture and antiquities to be found there. Frances' painting *Tarxien Lady* was inspired by megalithic carvings and sculptures found throughout Malta. She was fortunate to meet Marquis de Piro KM, who invited her to be Artist-in-residence in his palazzo, the Casa Rocca Piccola, in Valletta. During her time there she completed a series of watercolours of the interior of the palazzo as well as topographical paintings of the island. Frances' work made such a strong impression in Malta that she was included in the book *International Dictionary of Artists Who Have Painted Malta* by Nicolas de Piro.

Frances' interest in architecture and antiquities has also taken her to Turkey, a country that was, for centuries, conquered and settled by many different peoples. In Cappadocia, early Christians, like the Hittites before them, lived and worshipped in volcanic caves and painted primitive biblical scenes on the walls. These stimulated Frances' imagination and she produced a series of watercolours based on these cave paintings. In a later, safer period when people lived near the Bosphorus they built magnificently carved wooden houses, many of which are still standing. These buildings inspired Frances to create a series of etchings and monoprints entitled 'Ancient Artefacts' exploring the partnership between landscape and civilization.

The Haircut, linocut, 41.5 x 50cms

Lace Ladies, linocut, 41.5 x 50cms

Travel has been a constant source of inspiration, with images being recorded in her detailed sketchbooks. She regularly returns to Montreal and frequently visits Bermuda where her younger sister has lived for many years and where, again, Frances finds the visual stimulation that feeds her appetite for exploring and portraying different cultures. She has been invited to be Artist in Residence, in 2008, for the Masterworks Foundation in Bermuda with a solo exhibition of her work at the end of her three-month residency. On several occasions she has visited New Zealand where she was commissioned to paint a view of the city of Wellington

Swim, linocut, 43 x 57cms

Sunset Rhosneigr, oil, 40 x 60 cms

Surf, etching, 60 x 90 cms

and two farm landscapes.

Frances is inspired by the work of the American painter, Edward Hopper (1882-1967). Although Hopper's figures are commonly interpreted as 'lonely characters' Frances sees them as serene and peaceful. For her, Hopper captures a stillness in his work that has a meditative quality, with the figures simply showing their need to surround themselves with their own personal space. Another source of inspiration is the artist Alex Colville (b. 1920) who lives in Nova Scotia. Frances says 'I greatly admire the classical construction of Alex's work and the timeless quality of his paintings.'

Frances does not neglect the landscape and architecture of Great Britain. She is especially drawn to the brilliant light and rugged seascapes of Anglesey, where she spends considerable time. It was Rhosneigr beach in Anglesey that inspired *Surf*, the largest etching that Frances has ever produced. It was made with two large steel plates and printed in full colour. Managing to overcome the huge printing problems presented by its large scale, Frances made six prints, and says, 'Perhaps because of the struggle to produce this etching it has become one

Interior, Casa de Picola, Malta, watercolour, 36 x 28cms.
Private Collection

of my favourite pieces.'

Some of her most popular etchings have been based on subjects in Manchester, a city she has come to know and admire. Frances recalls her first visit to Manchester: 'my initial impressions were of a dark and gloomy, Dickensian city.' For many years she was on the Patrons Committee of Manchester City Art Gallery and experienced the transformation of the city into a vibrant, lively place in which to live and work. 'I especially like the combination of the regeneration of the old buildings with brand new modern buildings being built alongside. The city has such a buzz, and the confidence to put on fun events; I enjoyed designing a cow for The Manchester CowParade which was a great way to bring people into the city.'

As sketching on the spot in a busy city is a difficult option, she uses her camera to record the many images that interest her. In producing a piece of work, she may not faithfully replicate her photographs, instead combining elements from different photos to make a more interesting composition. The intricate ironwork of the city's old Victorian bridges appealed to Frances and resulted in her producing a series of etchings that celebrate the achievements of the industrial age in Manchester. The series consists of *Castlefield, Iron Bridges, Bridgewater Canal* and *Canal Basin.* Frances says, 'I come from an engineering family and really appreciate the beauty and the intricacy of these massive structures.' Frances also celebrated the achievements of the Victorian builders in her commission from Great Universal Stores to sketch a number of Victorian mills across Britain, two of which were chosen to be made into large paintings for their head office in London.

Frances' expertise at printmaking extends to the skilful linocuts she produces on her antique Albion press. Linocuts are a traditional form of relief printmaking, resulting in strong graphic images that are very much a part of Frances' background. An extremely complex form of linocut was used to produce an image of the library in Chester, which was printed in seven colours. Frances says

I used the method Picasso perfected called 'reduction prints' or 'suicide prints', so called because the artist starts with a full piece of lino, prints the first lightest colour, carves that away and prints the next colour, eventually arriving at a stage where nothing else can be carved away, having printed the darkest colour last. This leaves absolutely no margin for errors, but I think gives a much more lively and spontaneous image.

Her image of Chester Library is included in the book *Picturesque Chester, The City in Art* by Peter Boughton.

The linocut entitled *Swim* was produced after a visit to Bermuda; for this print, she used sandpaper on the plate to replicate the speckled look of the ground. The vacated deckchair casts a long shadow on the sizzling ground and the discarded sandals draw the viewer's eye to the sea. Another linocut, *Lace Ladies* depicts a typical street in Greece, where a row of old ladies, dressed in black, are making lace. Another print shows their men-folk passing the time of day at the outdoor barber's shop. In the monoprint entitled *Meeting Place* the rich, exotic colours capture the magical and mystical atmosphere that she experienced whilst travelling through Rajasthan, India. Frances has the enviable ability to absorb the culture of whichever country she visits and then impart, through various media, the sights, smells and sounds that are the essence of those places.

Frances' interest in all aspects of life throughout the world led her to help Poland during its troubled times in the early 1990s. She organised 'Art Aid'; a large exhibition of works by artists from the north west of England in order to raise enough funds to buy much needed supplies that were then sent, in three truck-loads, to Poland.

The largest exhibition of Frances' own work – at Salford Art Gallery in 1994 – consisted of approximately seventy five-pieces of work including oil paintings, watercolours, etchings, linocuts, monoprints, and drawings. During the exhibition Frances held workshops at the gallery for parties of schoolchildren and adults who were interested in printmaking.

In 1995 Frances became one of the founding members of 'Professional Artists in Cheshire', now known as 'Cheshire Artists Network' (CAN). Frances is on the committee and was instrumental in organising two of their biggest exhibitions: Warrington Museum in 1998 and the Williamson Art Gallery in 2001.

As an artist with an interest in architecture and antiquities she was asked to join the Board

Cat in the Undercroft, etching, 24 x 30cms

of Norton Priory Museum and Gardens, an archaeological museum in Halton, Cheshire, which was built on the site of a twelfth-century monastery. There, in 2005, she organised the 'Cat Walk' exhibition which consisted of forty concrete cats designed and painted by members of CAN and displayed throughout the gardens. The theme of cats was inspired by the Lewis Carroll connection with nearby Daresbury. At the end of the summer the cats were auctioned, raising a considerable amount of money for the local hospice.

There is a diversity in Frances' work which seems to emanate from her in-built curiosity and adventurous spirit. Underpinning all her work and the common thread that runs through it is her technical ability to draw. The huge pleasure she derives from drawing and printmaking has led her to disseminate these skills in the numerous workshops she has organised and run in schools, art galleries and museums over the past twenty years.

Frances feels that printmaking has been at the root of the diversity of her work, creating

Chester Library, linocut, 43 x 65cms

a struggle that forces her to re-think a subject. Enjoying the challenge that is intrinsic to this process has meant that her creativity has been constantly stretched so that her range of skills is both broad and deep. She says:

Printmaking for me is a way of exploring methods of making marks. The interaction of drawing, metal, and ink, I find exciting. There is also a robust satisfaction in preparing a plate for etching; carving away a piece of lino; rolling ink on a plate. While the mind is debating artistic problems the hands are actively engaged in practical problems; a combination I find physically exhausting but mentally stimulating.

White Jug, Black Boats, 2001, oil on board, 122 x 61cms. Private Collection

Sheila Meeks

Sheila Meeks was born in 1955 and lived in Stalybridge, Cheshire with her parents and two older sisters. She remembers a drawing she did as a young child of seven, which won a competition open to school children in the region. Inspired by the many family holidays in Anglesey, the drawing is of Lligwy Bay, the beach close to the farmhouse where they used to stay. Looking across the bay to a stone tower on a small island, the drawing shows a sophisticated skill. Executed in great detail, even down to their sunglasses, carefully placed groups of people sit in deckchairs protected from the elements by the windbreaks. Sheila recalls using her elder sister's oil paints for the first time when she was about nine years old.

Sheila wanted to be near the London galleries so chose to do her Fine Art Degree at Kingston University in Surrey. During that time she was inspired by a wide range of artists, visiting the National Gallery to enjoy the paintings of Piero della Francesca (c.1415/20–1492), and the Tate Gallery to study the painting technique of Georges Seurat (1859–1891) but also admiring the simplicity and symmetry of the minimal artist Frank Stella (b.1936) and the monochrome assemblage work of sculptor Louise Nevelson (1899–1988), which consisted of shallow box-like units filled with industrial waste wood. Sheila experimented with relief and collage work that spilled out of the rectangular frame, and considered surface texture and colour to be an important element of the final composition.

Using acrylics, she experimented with colour-field painting, enjoying the simplicity and objectivity of the pure bands of colour, a stark contrast to the more dominant trend of abstract expressionism. The beauty and power of using colours on a neutral background, and the way in which different colours behave, still informs Sheila's work.

After completing her degree at Kingston in 1977, Sheila was awarded the Picker Travel Scholarship to go to New York, where she recalls the excitement of seeing a huge variety of artists' work including those she had only previously seen in art books. The architecture in New York was another art form that Sheila had long admired.

In 1979, she spent five months in Paphos, Cyprus doing Post-Graduate Studies at Cyprus College of Art. Her work from this period centred around small reliefs using found objects from the Cyprus beaches. She also produced collages and mixed-media drawings to

Photo by Jennie Keegan

Yellow Road to the City, 2001, oil on board, 43 x 56cms. Private Collection

Jug and Bowl, 2002, oil on board, 43 x 54cms

Green Crane, Still Life, 2004,
oil on canvas, 108 x 83cms

Harbour, St Ives,
2004, oil on canvas,
33 x 38cms.
Private Collection

explore colour, texture, and composition. The work done in Cyprus culminated in a group show at The British Council in Nicosia.

On her return from Cyprus, Sheila spent a brief time in the south pursuing a career as an artist, before returning to Manchester in 1980 to study for a Post-Graduate Certificate in Art Education at Manchester University. In 1983 she joined MASA (Manchester Artists Studio Association) at their studios in Granby Row. Linda Weir, one of the founding members of MASA, organised a group trip to Cornwall where the artists revelled in the light, colour and scenery. Linda has since settled in St Ives and Sheila visits whenever she can, resulting in paintings that capture the raw beauty of the little Cornish harbours, one such painting entitled *Harbour, St Ives*.

In 1985 Sheila staged her first solo show at Oldham Art Gallery, resulting in many sales. In 1991 she had another solo exhibition, her first in London, at Le Chat Noir, in Convent Garden, where she was successful again in selling much of her work. Since then Sheila has exhibited at various public and private galleries throughout the country. In 2004, Sheila had her most successful exhibition to date at the Wendy J Levy Gallery in Manchester; a large percentage of the paintings were sold, with collectors coming from near and far to buy the work.

It was in 1991 that Sheila moved from South Manchester to live in Mossley where she was attracted by the stone buildings and hilly landscape that continue to inspire her, absorbing the atmospheric colours of the rugged landscape and incorporating them into her paintings.

Sheila enjoys working on a number of paintings at the same time, regaining a degree of spontaneity when moving from one piece to another. During the working process, she will begin by moving the paint freely around the surface of the canvas using a cloth or brush until the white of the canvas has been eliminated. This provides her with a base colour on which she is happy to work. During this process images from memory begin to emerge. The process can sometimes take many painting sessions but she knows it will eventually happen. The surface of the painting is of paramount importance, changing constantly during the course of its creation. The quality of the brush strokes, textures, colours and layers of paint are, in essence, her subject matter.

She places favourite objects such as lighthouses, flowers and fruit in such a way as to skilfully take the viewer on a journey through the painting. Along the way one sees the ghostly shapes lurking beneath the surface. These are the remnants of shapes or objects that Sheila has purposely painted over, adding layers of paint that create a visual depth. Such an example is *Jug and Bowl*, a painting of Sheila's kitchen table, with hints of hidden objects only just visible below the surface of the painting, adding a further subtle dimension to the work.

Yellow Road to the City, 2001, is one of Sheila's favourite paintings. A layering of paint was created through adding with a brush and taking off with a cloth, then adding a little more colour, creating a colour atmosphere that Sheila found very pleasing. The painting depicts the journey from the artist's home, past the row of cottages and up to the hazy and smoggy colours of the city in the distance.

Walking the Dog, 1998, oil on board, 31 x 36cms. Private Collection

With the birth of her son George in 1992, Sheila's work began to incorporate elements of her life with her child. Living a short distance from a park, a favourite pastime was to walk there looking at the world from the perspective of her son. *Plane and Cow for George* dated 1994, is a painting that incorporates, within the park, a cow, swings and plane as if seen from George's viewpoint. Predominantly painted in soft, hazy grey-pink tones, the colours are reminiscent of the shades of gravel along the pathway. With a high stone wall round the edge of the park, almost depicted as a frame on the left-hand side of the painting, the objects within it are seen as if looking through a window. One's eye then travels from left to right across the painting and takes in the row of terraced stone cottages where she and George live. Her use of the border or frame around the central section of a piece has evolved over the years. Using it initially almost as decoration, Sheila is more likely now to use the frame as a way to contain and control the objects within.

Small Flowers and Boats, also uses objects and pattern to lead the eye around the painting, but in this work the centre is left almost empty. Sheila's work over the years has become less 'busy', with empty spaces playing a key role in the composition. Compared to *Interior* painted much earlier in 1990, where the whole canvas provides visual stimulation, *Small Flowers and Boats* shows a more minimal quality.

In 1996 Sheila was awarded a Royal Bank of Scotland Award, by the Manchester Academy of Arts, for *Houses and Hills*, a small, elongated painting of a row of cottages in Mossley. A year later, with growing interest in her work, she was selected to show *Dark Hills, Red Clouds* at the Royal Academy Summer Exhibition in London which led to further opportunities to show her work at the Chelsea Art Fair.

Plane and Cow for George, 1994,
oil on canvas, 113 x 143cms

Winter Walk, 1997,
oil on canvas,
91 x 107cms

Small Flowers and Boats, 2001,
oil on board, 69 x 84cms.
Private Collection

Night Time Still Life, 2005,
oil on board, 23 x 28cms

Spring Flowers, Blue Jug, 2006,
oil on canvas, 55 x 64cms

In 1998, the respected art historian, Richard Kendal invited Sheila to show twelve small works at the Discerning Eye Exhibition in London. Included in the exhibition was *Walking the Dog*, one example of the small number of Sheila's paintings portraying the figure. *Winter Walk* painted in 1997 shows George and his father walking in the Mossley landscape. Nativity scenes, which Sheila feels may be inspired by her Catholic childhood, are other examples of her use of the figure.

Generally though, Sheila prefers not to incorporated figures within her paintings, fearing that the focus may become centred on the qualities of the specific figure. Even with a perfect model in her young son, the many sketches she produced never became paintings; they were simply an end in themselves.

Green Crane, Still Life, painted in 2004, perfectly juxtaposes two of Sheila's everyday scenes. In the top section of the painting is her view from the studio window, across to the building site on the other side of the road. At the forefront of the painting, depicting the studio interior, there is a table arranged with flowers and groups of fruit. The idea of painting the two elements together was triggered by the small jug which had been on the windowsill of her studio for many years. Built up in many thin layers of oil, the green apples on the table pick up the colour of the crane and the two oranges pick up the colour of the brickwork on the corner of the building seen from the studio window.

Views of landscapes through windows were quite common amongst a key group of modern-minded artists painting during the 1920s. The group was known as the Seven and Five Society, a founding member of which was Ivon Hitchens (1893–1979), an artist much admired by Sheila. Theirs was the concept of painting nature in an orderly and detached manner as if the landscape becomes part of the still life that often appears in the foreground. Sheila's painting *Night Time Still Life* shares Hitchens' concept, though her style is her own; looking out over the hills of Mossley, lights shine like beacons in the houses on the hill against the inky sky, the landscape integral to the still life of the interior.

White Jug, Black Boats demonstrates Sheila's more recent attraction to using brighter colours, and her love of the sea. Incorporating an interior, looking out to sea, the horizontal bands of table, floor and sea serve as a background to the objects set against them.

Autumn Flowers incorporates favourite objects set against the backdrop of the hills. The shapes and colours appear as if emerging naturally through the haze of the background.

Sheila's paintings are usually spontaneous; it is a rare occurrence for her to work from any preliminary materials but in her recent painting, *Spring Flowers, Blue Jug*, she was inspired by a photograph of the view from her kitchen window. The photograph was used as a starting

Dark Hills, Red Clouds, 1996, oil on canvas, 31 x 61cms. Private Collection

point but was not faithfully reproduced. Feeling that photographic references offer too much information and detail in which she can become stifled, she chose to reduce the contents of the photograph to its basic elements. Unusually, in this piece, she had a preconceived idea of what she wanted to paint.

Sheila likes the concept of allowing the objects in her paintings to float freely, without suggestion of perspective, thus enjoying the freedom to place objects in such a way as to improve the composition rather than positioning them where they would conventionally appear. She greatly admires the work of the Scottish artist, Craigie Aitcheson (b. 1926), one of whose paintings of his favourite dog, Wayney, also defies gravity; Wayney, having died, is seen ascending into the sky, paws first.

Another artist whose work has more recently received Sheila's admiration is Alfred Wallis (1855–1942), whose paintings produced a fresh, childlike style, employing bright colours and strong, rhythmic designs. Sheila's work has sometimes been likened to that of the naïve artists. However, this comparison has to be modified by her sophisticated use of colours, surfaces, balance and composition.

Sheila's work is in public and private collections in this country and abroad, including the Rutherston Loan Collection at Manchester Art Gallery and the prestigious Reader's Digest Collection in New York.

List of Subscribers

Barry Windle

David Goeritz

Keith Jeffery

David Hart

Sara Reston

Phil Livsey

Miles Clegg

Mrs A Snell

Peter Gannon

Jennifer A Johnson

James M Roark

Gordon Edwards

Lawrence and Liz Yusupoff

Joy Bamford

Roger and Pia Thelwell-Pichler

Angela McAlpine

Mrs. L De Turckheim

Rachel E Thompson

Vicki Buckmaster

Robert Godfrey

Jane Matthews

Judi and Malcolm Jayson

Caroline Humphries

Kate Eggleston-Wirtz

Kate French

John Paul Niemira

Brian Hanstein

Janet Lines

Mari Harper

Martin Littler

Walter and Ethel Lee

Walter and Mary Lee

William and Julie-Ann Lee

Charlie and Jacqueline Sowerby

Dr N and Mrs R Beenstock

Dr Angela Baird

Acknowledgements

This book has come to fruition with the help of several friends whom I would like to acknowledge. First of all I wish to thank my co-writer Judy Rose – without her invaluable work this book would not have been written. I also thank the artists for their enthusiastic involvement and input.

For their help in various ways including editing, contributions to text, and valued support, I would like to thank Jane Beenstock, Jennie Keegan, Nadege Guilera, Jonathan White, Hilary Jack, Amy Robinson, Ann Joseph and Fay Wertheimer.